# Detroit's Eastern Market

# Detroit's Eastern Market

## A Farmers Market Shopping and Cooking Guide

---

## Lois Johnson and Margaret Thomas

Photographs by Bruce Harkness

Montages and cover designed by the authors.

"Eastern Market Soup" recipe reprinted with permission from The More The Merrier!, © 1997, by the Hunger Action Coalition of Michigan.

ISBN 0-9676036-0-9

Printed by Baker Johnson Book Printing & Binding, Dexter, Michigan

# ❧ Contents ❧

# ❧ Acknowledgments ❧

We've met so many generous people since we began this project, that it would be impossible to mention them all. Besides Don and Marjorie Hirt's bird's-eye tour of the Market, and Ed Deeb's and Alex Pollock's enthusiasm for our story, we want to thank all the Market people who took the time to answer our questionnaire or be interviewed, often after a twelve-hour working day, for their patience and interest. Their spirit was always fresh and inspiring.

To all our friends and family members who read, edited, tasted, and encouraged, our warm appreciation. Words pale compared to Bruce Harkness's vibrant photographs, but thank you, Bruce, for enduring all the early hours and making the Market glow. The support and good humor of Chris and Jim made it all possible--our love and thanks.

Lois Johnson and Margaret Thomas
Detroit, 1999

# ❧ Preface ❧

Since the beginning of civilization, people have gathered in urban areas to buy, sell, trade, and barter foodstuffs. Even with the proliferation of supermarkets and vegetable/fruit mega-stores, most major U.S. cities still maintain a central farmers market. From New York to Los Angeles, New Orleans to Chicago, Seattle to Detroit to Boston, thousands buy their produce directly from the farmer who planted the seeds.

Like every automobile manufacturer, brokerage house or supermarket chain, American central markets have had their ups and downs, good years and slow ones. Eastern Market old-timers reminisce about the days in the first half of the century when 7,000 farmers came to Market every day to sell their produce. They traveled long distances, from all sections of Michigan, northern Ohio and Ontario, arriving in the middle of the night and sleeping in their trucks until the Market opened. There were so many of them that they had a one-stall limit rented in three-hour shifts. Their customers came in the family car, or by bus or foot; many did their own canning or putting-by for the Winter, and their only other food source was the corner grocery store, which often meant higher prices and limited variety.

After World War II, frozen foods, especially vegetables, became as commonplace in middle-class households as sliced bread. Everyone seemed to want convenience, and as more families had two working parents instead of one, fast-food and TV dinners became standard fare. But there has been a revival of interest in good food, and cooking is regaining its good name. Cooking shows, cook books, food columns, and food magazines abound. In the 1960's, Julia Child was one of the first to remind us how real, honest food tasted and how much fun it is to cook for ourselves and friends.

In the public's protest against pesticides and chemicals, organic farming has played an important role in the quest for good and nutritious foods. It has helped shape our awareness of how we fuel our bodies. Hopefully, it has made us more demanding of our food sources, so that we again care about eating fresh un-sprayed produce, free-range grain-fed poultry, and farm-fresh eggs. The foods and recipes in this book reflect the Eastern Market. They show the love and respect good food deserves. Many recipes come from generations ago--treasured family heirlooms still enjoyed today, some for everyday dinners, others for special celebrations.

When Margaret Thomas moved to Detroit from Florida in 1994, she fell in love with the Eastern Market. Although not an obsessive cook, she swoons at the sights and smells of a fine meal. This book is her idea. Living in the Market area, she shops there several days a week, calling a greeting to everyone in the Market, most by name, often stopping to chat about their families. A city person through and through, she thrives on the color and ambiance the Market exudes.

For Lois Johnson, a farmers market has provided serious food shopping since 1964, the first year she lived in Paris. After experiencing the pleasures of open-air shopping all over France and utilizing the wonderful and oldest market in England at Norwich, where else in Detroit could she go but Eastern Market? Johnson _is_ an obsessive cook, always planning a menu. Eastern Market has been her grocery store for thirty years.

Bruce Harkness, a photographer known for capturing the human spirit, gives us a record of Eastern Market today--the Market people, their products, and working place. His childhood memories of the Market illuminate his pictures.

There are many farmers markets across the country, markets with similar histories, businesses and devoted customers. But Eastern Market is Detroit's jewel, and we hope to give it a little shine.

The people--farmers, vendors, store owners, customers--are the core of the Market's life. They are the focus of this book. Through questionnaires, conversations, interviews, and observations we wanted to capture the personalities of these "food people." They have much in common--long days, early hours, the vagaries of the weather, and knowing they are essential to their community. They each have a different story to tell, a recipe to share.

# ◁ Origins ▷

In 1802, Detroit city officials established a central location for the marketing of agricultural goods. A municipal ordinance issued on March 20 of that year set aside riverside land at the foot of what would become Woodward Avenue for a new market that would be "highly useful, convenient, and beneficial to the vendor and purchaser of provisions." Foodstuffs from the shores of Michigan, Ontario, even Ohio moved to the town, rivaling the produce hauled overland by farmers. As riverfront real estate became more valuable with the diversification of port activities and Detroit's population burgeoned, the 1840's saw the Market relocate first inside Old City Hall, and later to a shed built for it on Cadillac Square--still owned by the city, establishing a pattern that would continue to the present.

The early nineteenth century saw today's Market area, with street names like Gratiot, Riopelle, St. Aubin, Orleans, and Rivard, farmed by French families such as Charles and Nicholas Guoin who laid claim to a fifty-five acre parcel just north of Gratiot Road, bounded on the west by Russell Street. In 1834, the City of Detroit purchased their land for $2,010. Thirty-five acres of the parcel were subdivided into lots and sold to German immigrants looking for a place to locate their community. The fifteen remaining acres that fronted Gratiot with Russell on the west side, became a second city cemetery. But by 1869, the cemetery was full and the City ordered the graves relocated in Grosse Pointe. As city growth, land values, and downtown congestion made the Cadillac Square market increasingly problematic (the "ladies" of the city

9

were appalled at the mess caused by the horse traffic and desired a more gracious place to shop for food), City officials moved the market north yet again, this time to the vacated cemetery land. Thus, in 1887, Detroit's open market moved to its present location and was renamed Eastern Market.

Just as street names reflect the Market area's French influence, so, too, do some of the buildings reflect its German heritage. Vivio's Restaurant is housed in Meyfarth Hall, built in 1892 for the German community as a social hall. Earlier, in 1875, Sacred Heart Church was consecrated at Eliot and Rivard to serve the German-Catholic population. Romanesque in style, with a 130-foot steeple, it remains a handsome structure that can be seen today from Interstate 75.

With its relocation to Russell Street and the building of its first municipal market hall, Eastern Market started to take shape. The first two sheds were put up in 1891. Shed #2 stands today surrounded by Russell, Winder, Market, and Adelaide Streets. By the turn of the century, many businesses were established on those streets.

After the First World War, to meet the increasing food demands of a growing city, more and more wholesalers and distributors settled in the Market district. To accommodate this growth, the City added more sheds, one in 1922 and another in 1929. As new businesses flourished, Eastern Market became the hub for southeastern Michigan food distribution. Shed #5 was added in 1938, and the last shed to be added was in 1965. To create parking space in the Market area, old Shed #1 was removed to Belle Isle and used there as a horse stable.

Originally, city planners developed three markets to fill the needs of its citizens: Eastern Market, Chene-Ferry Market, and Western Market. In 1965, Western Market and Eastern Market were consolidated. Chene-Ferry Market, mainly a produce terminal, no longer functions as a market, but is used as a recycling collection center.

In 1970, in an effort to bring consumers back to the city and the Market after the unrest of the 1960's, city architect, Alex Pollock, designed and painted colorful murals over the arched entrances to the sheds that have become Market logos over the years. The popularity of the new Market art prompted other owners to commission similar decorative motifs for their fronts, softening the austere nature of the solid brick buildings surrounding the Market.

Fire gutted Gratiot Central Market (located between Capital Poultry and Germack's on the Fisher Freeway Service Drive, fronting Gratiot Avenue) in August 1995. The loss of this prime shopping area in Eastern Market was felt by vendors and customers alike. Plans for rebuilding the massive one-story building were started before the year was out. When the new Central Market was near completion in 1998, murals were deemed an integral part of the restoration of the Gratiot Avenue facade. Artist Kim Fay, commissioned to create the murals, designed and installed eight trompe l'oeil panels depicting some of the vendors in the new structure.

The character of Eastern Market is a reflection of its origins and the changes it experienced over time. The State of Michigan declared the Market an historic site in 1977. Today, it is the center of trade for farmers from

Michigan, Ohio, Canada, and growers across the country
and, even though it has marks of the present, it looks in
many ways as it did a hundred years ago.

We have recounted the physical development of the
Market over the years, but the real story is told by the
families who started and continued the businesses in the
Market. Whether farmer, produce dealer, retailer,
wholesaler, or vendor, most of the businesses started as
family enterprises. These families grew up at the Market,
and their businesses passed from one generation to the
next.

Throughout our book you'll find stories and recipes
from customers' families as well, often two but many of
three or four generations, who still shop faithfully at
Eastern Market. Rose Marie Nemerski Mason remembers:

> My earliest recollections are those of a
> small, seven year old girl whose tall father
> held on to her small hand. Mother would
> have my brothers in a wagon or they would
> walk along as well. Elie was five and
> one-half, and Michael about four. Mother
> says we always went together to the "Big
> Market" (Gratiot Central) for fish that
> were still alive with their shiny skins and
> eyes. We bought meat in that huge place,
> too. Spices were in the center area.
>
> In the open Market, tables with stacks of
> seasonal vegetables seemed very long and I
> had to look upwards to see them. We
> bought tomatoes in the canning season, even

though we had a big garden at home. Mother canned about two hundred quarts of tomatoes each year which she used for soup, spaghetti, and various Polish and Romanian dishes.

We bought live poultry at the Market, chicken, duck for czarnina soup and turkey for the holidays. The live poultry was all over the Market, chicks chirping, ducks quacking. The ducks and turkeys were brought home live, and we kept a few in the garage area. The czarnina soup was made with blood freshly taken from the duck or turkey before baking. There were bunnies too, as there are today. I am still an enthusiastic fan of the Market.

Detroit's Eastern Market is the largest open-air wholesale/retail market of its kind in the United States. Specialty shops, bakeries, spice companies, meat and poultry markets, restaurants, jazz cafés, old-time saloons, produce firms, gourmet shops, truck-farm sheds, cold-storage warehouses, and parking areas span over three square miles. More than 150 food-related businesses are operating in the Market area as we enter the twenty-first century.

Many products in today's Market are native to Michigan soil. In the eighteenth century, Mme de Cadillac delighted in finding wild berries and fruits, while melons, beans, and other vegetables were cultivated by Native

## Origins

Americans long before the French docked on Detroit's shores. Forests were home to wild bees making honey, still a large Michigan crop, and Michigan maple trees supplied enough sap to produce over fifty thousand pounds of maple sugar as early as 1819.

In the middle of the nineteenth century, as immigrants came westward with the opening of the Erie Canal, ethnic communities began to shape Detroit into a major city. Eastern Market reflects this variety of cultures and traditions, giving it a vitality only experienced by walking through its many streets and sheds. The design of the Market is organic, growing out of a city's needs.

# ❧ Market Seasons ☙

Following the garden's calendar year 'round develops seasonal eating habits. Tastes become conditioned by what farmers offer. Shopping at a farmers market provides the perfect venue for healthier and more creative cooking. Imagination and taste buds are sparked by the smells and colors of fresh, just-picked produce.

## Spring

In early spring, the senses are awakened by the new fruits and vegetables that appear in the stalls. Rhubarb, a Michigan hot-house specialty, comes packed in boxes like long-stemmed roses. Pencil-thin asparagus, sweet sugar snaps, tender peas, crisp radishes, green onions, and spinach arrive. Distant southern growers supply oranges, blueberries, raspberries, broccoli, and hot-house tomatoes. Damp spring weather brings the mushroom season. Michigan morels, with their honey-combed caps, are highly prized.

By early June, Michigan strawberries, sweet and red to the center, are plentiful. Everyone has a flat balanced on their carts. Tender local lettuces and herbs also make the scene by then.

## Summer

The warm summer sun brings abundance and variety to the Market. Crunchy green beans and cucumbers and early baby summer squashes fill rows of little wooden baskets.   Michigan cherries and blueberries, precious blackberries, and raspberries appear.

Vine-ripened melons are piled on the tables in late July. Honey Rocks are a Michigan thumb-region specialty. Peaches and golden apricots from southwestern Michigan compete with the Leelanau area's dark sweet cherries.  By August, endless varieties of eggplant, squash, onions, peppers, and fresh herbs fill the air with their pungent aromas.  At Eastern Market, really fresh sweet corn is picked just before dawn on Market day.

As summer moves along, it's hard to resist big baskets brimming with luscious, ripe tomatoes.  Over thirty kinds are grown in Michigan.  Since the most economical way to purchase tomatoes is by the bushel, it is time to start canning.

## Fall

In autumn, the Market takes on a burnished splendor with apples, pears, pumpkins, and winter squashes. Michigan ranks second nationally in apple production. Washington grows more, but Michigan outdoes it in range. There are sixty varieties now and new ones come to the Market each year.  Some of the choicest ones grown in Michigan are McIntosh, dark red Cortland, semi-tart Jonathan, Red and Golden Delicious, Jonagold, Gala, Ida Red, Northern Spy, Mutsu, and green Granny Smith.

Ciders produced from these apples are as varied and delicious as the apples themselves.  Cider makers have their own blends and no two taste the same.  High in vitamin C and fiber, fat-, sodium-, and cholesterol-free, cider has only 120 calories per 8-ounce glass.

Pears crowd in between the tables of apples.

September offers a second chance for raspberries, often more flavorful than the earlier summer ones.

## Winter

With colder weather, the open air sheds begin to close down, but a few hearty souls brave the elements.

In the covered sheds, life goes on almost as usual. Root vegetables are this season's mainstay. Long stalks of Brussels sprouts catch the eye. Multiple varieties of potatoes and winter squashes appear, as do rutabagas, turnips, parsnips, and carrots. Savoy cabbages, with their queenly ruffs, hold court.

Many regulars are there and so are the pork butchers. Refrigerated cases full of fresh bacon, ribs, chops, even heads, tails, ears, and trotters signal winter. This is the place and time to shop for sausage making.

The winter holidays bring a brisk business to Market retailers. Cars crowd every nook and cranny of the Market. A steady stream of traffic moves up, down and around Russell, Winder, Market and Adelaide.

After the New Year, the Market settles down to a more tranquil pace, except for the wholesale businesses, which continue year round. The plant growers seem to take a well-deserved break from the Market during the first three months of the year, but they're really gearing up for Easter, making sure tulips and lilies are at their flowering peak.

## Spring again--the Flower Growers

Eastern Market Flower Day is Detroit's rite of Spring. Since 1966, on the third Sunday in May, flowers take over the three square miles of Market space. Six-foot racks filled with flats of annuals crowd the streets, parking lots, and sheds. Alyssum to zinnias, hundreds of vendors sell their flats to thousands of flower lovers.

Spring is here again, proclaimed by flats of mandarin-red geraniums, orange marigolds, and yellow pansies. Cries of "How much for this flat?", "Can I mix a flat?", "Here's a better deal!" are heard across and down the aisles--aisles crowded with the shoppers' wagons, wheelbarrows, and homemade-carts. Lemonade stands, colossal barbecue grills with rows of shish-kabobs, brats, Polish sausages, booths with onion rings, elephant ears, funnel cakes, ice cream cones, snow cones, and cotton candy make it easy for shoppers to revive their energy. Blues musicians, reggae bands, saxophone players, and guitar music fill the Market. Combine all this and flowers, too, for a glorious Flower Day.

But flowers at Eastern Market aren't just a one-day affair--they're a year-round business. Throughout the twelve months, Eastern Market sells an amazing variety of plant life. According to Market Master Jesse Henderson, from April to July, bedding plants account for the largest sales of the Market, with Flower Day in May the premier showcase.

Fresh-cut flowers are always in Shed #3, as are full-sized, thriving house plants and cacti. The last two Sheds are filled almost entirely with nursery growers' stalls.

All spring and summer, perennials line the aisles with healthy, vigorous specimens--astilbes, heathers, rhododendrons, roses, graceful clematis. Bushes, shrubs, ornamental trees, and yews abound. Flats of vegetable seedlings, ready to plant in late May, are hardy and well-rooted.

By July, when the annual planting season winds down, the flower growers go back to their greenhouses to start next year's crop.

As fall approaches, many of these vendors embellish their stalls with fancy autumn arrangements of gourds, dried flowers, and decorative autumn wreaths. Mums in orange, golds, and reds, and well-rooted perennials line the walkways for fall planting.

From Thanksgiving to the New Year, Christmas trees, wreaths, cemetery blankets, and poinsettias fill the back sheds and parking lots. Find these robust vendors by the smoke of their coal burners. Evergreens and festive decorations take over the sheds and the stores bustle.

# ∞ Market Businesses ∞

## Shops

Our guide to the stores starts with R. Hirt and continues around the periphery of the Market sheds, going south along Market Street, turning west along the Fisher Freeway Service Drive, and finally going north up Russell.

> R. Hirt Jr. Company
> 2468 Market Street
> 313.567.1173
> hours: Tues-Fri 8am-5pm; Sat 7am-4pm

Shoppers who crowd into Hirt's on Saturday mornings go primarily for the finest selection of cheeses in the city, over 300 varieties, imported and domestic. They find old-world charm at the long wooden counter embellished with Pewabic Pottery tiles, where they queue up in front of knowledgeable vendors. Behind that counter, a walk-in refrigerator holds the cheeses plus patés, salamis, and other cured meats, butter, and eggs.

One can browse and shop before getting in line at the cheese counter. Head for the third floor via the old, wooden stairway at the back of the store (the second floor, now a storage area, once served as the home of the original Hirt family). Wicker fills the third floor, from party-favor-sized baskets to chairs and tables; gift items, plus a line of Michiganian crafts are here, too, taking on the look of the current season from New Years to Christmas.

On the first floor, pick up a hand-held basket (no room for carts here), and scan the shelves and pallets stocked with comestibles--oils, vinegars, mustards, jams, coffee and teas, crisp breads and cookies, tinned fishes, pastas and rices, dried fruits and nuts, candies.

At the cheese counter, nibble some samples, order your cheeses (one pound minimum and no slicing), and have your bills of lading written up (you get separate ones for foods and non-foods). Pay at the European-style cashier's cage. The lines may be long, but they buzz with food talk.

Established in 1887 by Rudolph Hirt, Hirt's functions primarily as a wholesaler to restaurants and grocery stores. On a week-day morning, flat-bed carts filled with orders for the city's best restaurants crowd the aisle and the lines aren't as long to buy your pound of Vermont cheddar or Bulgarian Feta. David DeVries, great-grandson of R. Jr., is always busy, but never too busy to chat about Hirt's and its history. He explains,

> R. Hirt was not a "Jr." There was an uncle in the city by the same name and in order to keep their mail separate, the younger R. Hirt adopted the Jr.

In spring and summer, the sidewalk area in front of the store displays outdoor and garden items, mainly terra cotta and stone pots for all those plants bought on Flower Day.

> Cost Plus Wines
> 2448 Market Street
> 313.259-3845
> hours: Mon–Fri 8:30am-6pm; Sat 7am-4:30pm

Cost Plus wines carries a large selection of fine wines, plus a wide choice of American and English beers. Tim McCarthy and his son, Dan, help in making the right selection.

In 1983, Tim opened his wine shop in Eastern Market. This corner space, originally a warehouse, was gutted and renovated by the McCarthy's. Tim says, in his Irish cadence,

> I've been here since St. Patrick's Day of '83. I have always loved the Market. There was no wine shop here, but lots of walking traffic and people interested in good food, so I thought good food and wine just complement each other. I don't know of a better or safer place than the Market to have a business.

Back-to-back cases of wine, arranged by country of origin, form the aisles of the shop. Wall shelves are filled to the brim, and Tim's hand-printed signs give helpful descriptions of the wines.

Capital Poultry
1466 E. Fisher Freeway
313.567.8200
hours: Tues-Sat 8:30am-5pm

In 1927, when Lillian Licata Arnone was born, her father, Tony Licata, started his poultry market on Gratiot and Vernor in a space rented from the Germack family. He called it Capital Poultry, "spelled with an 'A'."

After extensive remodeling and modernizing, today's customers are served from a center aisle, running front to back, with long refrigerated counters on each side. Midway down the aisle at the ordering, weighing, and paying area, you can catch a glimpse of your poultry being prepared on stainless steel tables.

Capital buys their fryers, roasters, and capons from Amish farmers in northeastern Indiana. These free-range chickens are totally grain-fed. The turkeys are raised in southeastern Michigan, the best he can buy, says Al Arnone, Lillian's son, who operates the Gratiot store.

Poultry comes in live (except for ducks and rabbits) in wooden crates and all the preparation is done on the premises. During Thanksgiving week, Arnone's turkey population jumps to over 2,000, and they work around the clock getting them ready.

Arnones opened a warehouse on the north side of the freeway in the '90's, meeting Federal guidelines to sell wholesale. Larry Arnone, another son, runs the warehouse.

Lillian talks fondly of the days when Vernor Highway (now the Fisher Freeway), was a street-level thoroughfare with a stop light and a policeman.

During the war, throngs of people came to the Market. This was long before the freeway came in and divided it. There was a communal feeling. We had a stall in Shed #1 until 1954 and sold live chickens, three for a $1.

---

Gabriel Importing Company
2461 Russell Street
313.567.2890
hours: Mon-Sat 8am-4pm

---

For an adventure in Middle Eastern cuisine, Gabriel's offers olives, salads like tabouli and fatoush, hummus, many varieties of feta cheese, and breads--pita, lavash, and mancosh b zaather, an herb bread.

Step to the back of the store for the wide assortment of imported olives kept in five-gallon white tubs: dry Moroccan, Calamatas and green Sicilians, and the special house-spiced green ones. Ladle them into the plastic containers provided.

A long, narrow shop with only one aisle, the walls are lined with shelves holding the largest stock of imported olive oils in the Market and a fine array of spices, including a bin of scarlet pomegranate powder, known as sumac in some parts of Lebanon.

Michael Sandros owns and runs Gabriel Importing. Born in Lebanon, of Greek extraction, he bought the store in 1990. On Saturdays, Sandros is helped by other family members: Maria, his sister-in-law; her son Nicolas; and her daughter Marinella.

This Middle Eastern emporium features Shangleesh, a yogurt cheese, made locally. Rolled in cumin-based herbs and spices, it is made only in cool weather when the yogurt can be drained at the proper temperature.

---

Rocky Peanut Company
2489 Russell Street
313.567.6871
hours:  Mon-Fri 7am-5pm; Sat 7am-5pm

---

First located at the corner of the Fisher Freeway Service Drive and Russell, Rocky Peanut Company moved one block north to its current location in 1981. Originally built by Rocco Russo as a wholesale produce warehouse, at the City's urging he converted it to a retail space.

Rocky bought his original peanut house at the Fisher Freeway Service Drive and Russell in 1969. That building now contains Johnnie Mack Cookie Factory, Flat Planet Pizza, Gabriel Importing, Russell Street Deli, and Zef's Coney Island at street level, while the second floor was converted into artist-loft apartments, a model for later ones in the area.

Stainless steel see-through shelves fill the center on the right side of the store holding Indian, Thai, Chinese, Italian, and Mexican staples, plus honeys, jams, European baking mixes, unusual oils (like grapeseed and pistachio), imported crackers and cookies, and an impressive stock of dried pastas. Many items are imported, but others are from small local companies that Rocky promotes. The City Farm label, their own line, depicts Eastern Market as a farm within the city.

Along the back wall, plastic bins hold grains, dry legumes, spices, and other baking needs. To the right, the glass counter displays dried fruits and nuts, followed by deli meats and cheeses, domestic and imported. Keep moving toward the smell of cinnamon-roasted almonds. Next come fresh, house-made carry-out sandwiches and salads.

The other half of the store is the ultimate up-date of the old penny-candy shop. By rough estimate, there are over 400 kinds of bite-sized candies--hard, soft, chewy, gooey, even sugar-free. This side also stocks coffees and teas and has an inviting little sit-down coffee bar.

As the store's name suggests, one can buy some fine peanuts here. The humble mainstay of any diet, peanut butter, is ground fresh, with or without salt.

---

Rafal Spice Company
2521 Russell Street
313.259.6373
hours: Mon-Sat 7am-4pm

---

"I don't smell anything, not a thing. The bankers love it because the money smells like spices!" says Donald Rafal. "I'm glad my father wasn't in the fish business." Spices and herbs, coffees and teas give Rafal's its heady bouquet. Rafal finds his store comfortable and the rent is cheap. His grandfather had owned the premises since the 1920's.

Brightly labeled bottles, boxes, and bags, each containing an elixir to perk up any concoction, line the shelves. Glass jars are filled with every spice and herb imaginable, from adobo and asafetida to xanthan and za'atar. To the left of the spice area, canisters of teas and kegs of coffee beans lend their fragrances.

Behind the cash register, Rafal sells an interesting and comprehensive assortment of pepper mills, and a wide selection of pepper-oriented spice mixes.

Donald Rafal explains,

> Rafal is from Rafalsky. When my grandfather came over from Russia, at the turn of the century, immigration officers shortened our name. We say Rafal, like the ticket, raffle ticket.

---

Eastern Market Bagel Factory
2534 Market Street
313.396.5558
hours: Mon-Fri 3am-3pm; Sat 3am-4pm

---

As if Geray Fermanis isn't busy enough with his Farmers Restaurant, he also owns a bagel factory next door. The bagels are mixed and baked right on the premises, "real" bagels, no fat, cooked the old-fashioned way--first simmered in boiling water then baked.

Clear glass bins hold the bagels: sesame, parmesan, garlic, onion, everything, salty, as well as a tempting pick of donuts, and cold drinks or coffee to go.

Both Farmers and the Bagel Factory are open Monday through Saturday. What does Geray Fermanis do on Sunday? "I am a bee keeper. I have about fifty-three bee hives on my farm, and I harvest about 6,000 lbs. of

honey a year. It relaxes me. It is all wooded, very quiet."
His honey is for sale at Farmers.

## Restaurants

*Market* area restaurants serve well-prepared foods any time of the day. Bacon and eggs or fettuccini carbonara, lunch-counter service or linen table cloths, the choices are tempting.

| |
|---|
| Russell Street Deli<br>2465 Russell Street<br>313.567.2900<br>hours: Mon-Fri 11am-2:30pm; Sat 8am-2:30pm |

At lunchtime, this long, narrow forty-five-seat diner bulges with hungry people. Bob Cerrito's food approach is seasonal and it shows in his soups, salads and daily specials.

He remembers coming to the Market as a youngster

with my grandparents and parents. One of my most vivid memories was a vendor who gave me a pear, a ripe pear and said, 'eat this and tell your parents how good it was'. I've always enjoyed the things that the vendors would say when trying to advertise their produce. They can be tremendously funny.

With his restaurant right in the Market, he can get that ripe pear at its peak. Cerrito scouts the stalls early in the morning, looking for anything special, buying the best fruits to make his breakfast pancakes, popular with Saturday Market shoppers.

---

Flat Planet Pizza
2457 Russell Street
313.567.7879
hours:  Tues-Sat 11am-4pm

---

One door south of Russell Street Deli is Bob Cerrito's pizza shop. He mixes this small space with works by local artists.

Cerrito searches for the perfect pizza crust.

My Sicilian grandmother showed me how to make bread when I was ten. Every week she would take five pounds of flour and change it into bread, and give each of her children a loaf on Sunday--a family ritual.

Her pizza was astounding. She baked them on a rectangular sheet pan--a little thick by American standards, yet a very delicate crust and heavy on the olive oil--a lot of olive oil in the pan, a lot of olive oil on the top and not much sauce. She peeled fresh tomatoes over a sieve, letting most of the juice drain out, and scattered the pulp and some finely minced onions around on top of the oil. Her pizzas were really sparse, compared to American pizza with its thick layers of cheese. It came out of a peasant tradition of living frugally.

Our family's approach to food has been to season things. Meat was not a main course, it was a seasoning. To put some salt and oil on the pasta was enough.

Salads, drinks, and desserts plus Bob's pizza make a great evening with no cooking. Call in advance, and Cerrito and staff will cater your parties.

---

Butcher's Saloon
1489 Winder
313.567.4999
hours: Mon 7am-8pm; Tues-Sat 7am-10pm

---

About the time Rudolph Hirt, Jr. bought the white clapboard house on Market Street, Dominique Riopelle, Jr. was building his saloon just down the block on Winder. Set in stone above Butcher's doorway is the date 1883. In 1903, Butcher's was listed in the Detroit City Directory as a saloon, but the second floor also had overnight guest rooms for farmers after busy Market days and for theatre buffs who wanted to stay downtown after an evening of entertainment. In its checkered history, the upstairs provided space for a bordello and a bookie operation (the telephone wires still exist) while, downstairs, the owners served great food as they do today.

Breakfast is served all day "with all the freshness and quality of the Eastern Market"-- French Toast soaked in cream and eggs and laced with Grand Marnier, and jumbo Omelets with all the trimmings. Butcher Burgers and Corned Beef Sandwiches, featuring Wigley's famous meats, add to the lunch menu.

The Saloon is a popular hangout for sports-minded Market workers and customers.

```
Vivio's Restaurant
2460 Market Street
313.393.1711
hours:  Tues-Thurs 11am-8pm;
        Fri 11am-9pm; Sat 7am-3pm
```

John Vivio's customers enjoy his good food and collection of antiques and Market memorabilia. Beautiful wooden doors from an Indiana Amish horse-drawn bread truck, porcelain dolls, pre-Prohibition liquor bottles, a few deer heads, and wagon wheels adorn the walls. "Most of the artifacts hanging on these walls were given to me by patrons, like the wood French clarinet from a sales manager at Wolverine Packing."

Vivio says many families have been in the Market longer than his, but he boasts over twenty six years and maintains that his building is the oldest to operate continuously as a tavern in the city of Detroit. Built in 1892, "Meyfarth Hall" is chiseled above the restaurant's entrance. The first level housed a tavern, the second the Meyfarth family quarters, and the third a meeting hall for the German community in the area.

Vivio's fare comes from family recipes. John recalls, "When we were growing up, Sunday was a big day for the family meal. My dad made all the pasta, his own ravioli, and potato gnocchi. "

John Vivio does most of his own cooking and prep work, starting early each morning. Today's menu includes Pasta with Italian Sausage, Chicken Piccata, Veal Marsala, Roasted Peppers, Calamari, Artichokes Alfredo, and terrific Mussels Marinara, as well as standard breakfast and lunch choices.

---

Roma Cafe
3401 Riopelle
313.831.5940
hours: Mon-Fri 11am-10pm; Sat 11am-midnight

---

Wood-paneled rooms and tuxedoed waiters give the Roma Cafe an old-world charm and elegance. Its menu lives up to the setting. Extensive and comprehensive, it offers appetizers from a simple tomato and fresh mozzarella salad to roasted peppers or crispy, lightly battered calamari. The pastas range from a delicate hay and straw Alfredo to rich lasagna. Veal, chicken, lamb, and fish, with sauces from Northern to Southern Italy--all are done to order. Cannolis, southern style, add the final touch. A long wine list complements the menu.

The Roma Cafe is an extended-family establishment, started in the 1920's by the Sossi family from Turin, Italy. The Sossis purchased the building on Erskine from the Marazza family who had run a boarding

house there since 1888.  The Marazzas offered room and board to farmers from the western and northern reaches of Michigan who came to the Market selling their wares. Signora Marazza's "board" was so fabulous that she was persuaded to open a restaurant.  Today, three generations later, the restaurant, named the Roma Cafe by the Sossis, is run by Janet Sossi Belcoure, the grandniece and granddaughter of the original owners.

Hands-on family management keeps the Roma a successful restaurant, says Belcoure.  Her mother, maternal aunt, and cousins work there.  Now it's Janet's turn.

---

Farmers Restaurant
2542 Market Street
313.259.8230
hours:  Mon-Fri 3am-2:30pm; Sat 3am-4pm

---

Geray Fermanis opened his Farmers Restaurant on November 15, 1975.  With two kitchens, one for each seating area, each with its own team of cooks and waiters, but both from the same menu, you may wait in line on the sidewalk, but once you're in, the service is fast and the food is good.

Fermanis was out there on the sidewalk, too, in those early days, meeting his potential customers, introducing himself, finding out what they liked.

I learned over the years what to do.  Your customer gives you that experience.  You never know who you are going to meet.  And

I talk to everybody.  The Eastern Market is a community.  There is no doubt in my mind that it is the safest place to have a business.

Fermanis offers over twenty omelets.  The fresh pan sausage is ground especially for Farmers, using the sweet meat that comes from pork neck.  Three people keep up the supply of freshly peeled potatoes for hash browns and home fries.

Like many others, Farmers Restaurant building, at the corner of Market and Adelaide, was a boarding house for farmers at the turn of the century.  In the 1930's it served as a banana warehouse.  The hooks still hang in the basement where the bananas were cured, and on the Adelaide Street side you can see the trap door where the fruit was dropped through.  It became a restaurant in 1958.

Today, it houses one of the most popular eateries in the Market.  Besides the prodigious breakfast menu, Farmers offers sandwiches, salads, and daily specials like stir fries and fish and chips.

---

Zef's Coney Island
2469 Russell Street
313.259.4705
hours:  Mon-Fri 5:30am-3:30pm; Sat 5:30am-4pm

---

The Coney, a deluxe-style hot dog, is a Detroit tradition, and Zef's is a Market one, popular with all members of the workforce.  With a melting pot clientele, Zef's enjoys the success that comes with good food, a quick meal, a short lunch break, or a breakfast of farm-fresh scrambled eggs and the house-special hash browns. No frills here, this is a true diner with clattering dishes, flatware, cups, and glasses as sparkling as the conversation of the customers, an all-American lunch counter.

# ⚞ Market Wholesale Dealers ⚟

## Produce

By rough count, there are twenty-five to thirty produce dealers located in the Market area. In the early morning hours, they select the best from the Produce Terminals to supply the restaurants and grocers in the Metro area. A few sell in the Saturday Market, often from more than one stall, in the East to West aisles of the sheds. They provide out-of-season fruits and vegetables as well as the pick of the current season.

---

Charlie Palazzolo & Sons, Inc.
2611 Russell Street

---

Dominic Palazzolo heads this family business, established four generations ago. It started with his maternal grandfather, one of the Lopiccolo brothers, a family of produce dealers. Both families came from Sicily.

All my kids worked in the Market on Saturday. I had to do the same thing with my father when I was young. I couldn't miss a Saturday. I don't think I missed three Saturdays until I was drafted into the service. During the week we sell wholesale, but on Saturdays we have several stalls for retail out in the sheds. There was a time when the main source of livelihood for my Dad was the Saturday Market.

Dominic's children, Julie and Frank, represent a new generation in the Market.

---

**Vitale Watermelon & Plants**
**2801 Russell Street**

---

In his office in the Fort Street Produce Terminal, Jim Vitale, often called "the Watermelon King," keeps Eastern Market memorabilia at hand.

Vitale, who took over his father's business in 1946, helped establish higher standards for the watermelon industry, eliminating #2 grade watermelons, calling for higher sugar content, uniformity, and better shipping regulations. Before, watermelons were arbitrarily thrown on a truck, any size, shape, and number with little concern for character or flavor.

From mid-April to the end of September, you can get a choice watermelon from Vitale's on Russell Street at the corner of Alfred. Early spring watermelons are brought in from Mexico, Georgia, Florida, and Texas. In September, the Michigan watermelon takes its place among the others. Vitale says a watermelon ripens in sixty to sixty-five days in the south and seventy to eighty days in Michigan.

He sells about forty-eight loads of watermelons a season, 2,500 melons a load. At the terminal in peak season, he averages twenty-five loads a day, about 500 loads a season.

---

**Mercurio Brothers, Inc.**
**2900 Rivard**

Joe Mercurio has been on Rivard since July 1, 1975. His father, Jacko, with his brothers, John and Frank, had established Mercurio Brothers at 12th Street and Rivard, near the produce terminal in 1924. They began with bananas and general produce, but in 1937 decided to specialize in bananas, because "they have appeal."

Mercurio's warehouse is spotless, reflecting the care that is given their product. "Don't keep bananas in plastic bags. Store them in a cool place, but not the refrigerator, if you want them to keep longer. Let the air circulate. Best of all is to eat them." His favorite way is to top a nice ripe banana with peanut butter.

Joe's office holds a collection of banana memorabilia and lots of family pictures. One in particular, of a family reunion, shows everyone gathered together smiling happily in their bright banana-yellow tee shirts. Why?, because "they have appeal."

---

**DelBene Produce**
**2501 Russell Street**

Angela DelBene grew up with the Market.

My grandfather was in the wholesale business where the Fisher Freeway is now, and he always had a stall in the Market on Saturdays. My Dad had a stall in the Market, too. All the kids helped out.

When she married, DelBene thought that would be the last of her Market days. Widowed at an early age, she raised her five children. In 1990, they all returned to the Market and established DelBene Produce.

DelBene services mostly restaurants. They also have a double stall on Saturday at the northwest end of the first shed where they sell top-grade citrus fruits, grapes and well-chosen vegetables at good prices. Their bright yellow and blue facade on Russell is easy to spot.

| |
|---|
| Ciaramitaro Brothers Produce<br>2506 Market Street |

Since he was six years old, Sal Ciaramitaro has been a champion of Detroit's Eastern Market. His grandfather, from Terrecini on the Palermo coast, founded the company over seventy-five years ago. Back then, Sal would help his grandfather with the customers, and he learned the business. He has vivid recollections of what the Market was like in the 1920's.

> The farmers would come down with their horses and wagons and bring their food. The building next to mine where the bank is, was a hay loft where the farmers stabled their horses and slept in the hay above it. All the streets in that area were cobblestone. We had 700-800 farmers every week day. We had a Saturday Market, too, but the farmers were there

everyday and they were ninety percent of
the Market.

Ann Ciaramitaro, Sal's wife, keeps the company
books.   When you walk up the entrance ramp of the
warehouse, her office is to the right and Sal's to the left
where he still writes all his invoices by hand.  Like others of
his generation in the Market, he maintains a personal touch
with his clientele.
   In good weather, you often hear music on the
sidewalk in front of Ciaramitaro's, one time a jazz combo,
the next a reggae group.

Our building was constructed with wooden
pegs.  We have tried to preserve it as much
as possible.   It had been John Brown's
hideaway for the slaves, and there is a
tunnel that leads to Busy Bee Hardware on
Gratiot.  It is like a honeycomb down there.

---

Tom Maceri & Sons
2820 Rivard

Tom Maceri is proud of his hard-working family.
His sons and son-in-law, daughter and daughters-in-law
share the business with him.  "I guess you have to be born
into this business to take the hours," says Maceri.
   Tom remembers his first experience in the Market.

The Trugali brothers' father was across the street from Ciaramitaro's. Upstairs they had a tomato room and they would also bunch celery, twelve to a bundle. I used to go up and watch them. That was over sixty-five years ago.

A photo of their first customized and brightly painted delivery truck made in 1948 hangs in the office next to the phone which never stops ringing.

## Meat

To the east of the Market sheds, streets like Riopelle are lined with meat packers and wholesalers. Others are located to the north and east where their plants and fleets of trucks find more open space. Only a few sell retail from their warehouses.

| Wolverine Packing Company |
| 2535 Rivard |

"My dad always had a piece of calf skin tacked on the front of his desk. When we moved into our new offices (April 1990), I did not want to forget from whence we came." Jim Bonahoom's modern, streamlined buildings reflect the new directions his company has taken, but the cowhide-fronted desk and his father's gold pens remain.

Wolverine's plant dominates the west flank of the Market along Rivard with its fleet of fifty yellow, white and black semis.

Jim Bonahoom serves on many organizations dedicated to the development and future of the Market. Although he sees the Market primarily as a wholesale business venue, he wants "the charisma and earthiness of the produce and retail market preserved. The interdependent nature of the food industry, the necessity of getting along with your neighbors, creates a close-knit environment."

---

General Provisions Inc.
2931 Russell Street

---

Ralph Brummer gets excited when he talks about Eastern Market. He has been in the Market "forever" and is dedicated to its success.

Brummer's first General Provisions Inc., a small, narrow shop carrying a full line of meats, but specializing in goat meat, stood at the foot of Russell just north of where the expressway is today. In the 1970's, he moved farther north up Russell. "We're an old type of butcher shop where you go in and ask for a specific cut of meat, and we cut it like the customer wants, the old fashioned way."

Market Wholesale Dealers _____

> Cattleman's, Inc.
> 1825 Scott

Markus Rohtbart, Chairman of Cattleman's, Inc., a family-owned wholesale beef processing company, came to America in 1949 from Poland at age twenty-three. A year later, he founded Cattleman's on a "shoe-string" and has built it into a company with over 260 employees.

Although Cattleman's is a wholesale company, a small retail shop operates in front of the long low plant, a good place to get large beef ribs and a bottle of Billy Bones B.B.Q. Sauce, a sauce as "bodacious" as the label advertises. Cattleman's has other retail stores throughout the metropolitan area.

> Wigleys Meat
> 1537 Hale

The label on the Wigleys Corned Beef package tells us "the Wigley family has a history of fine meats and meat recipes that spans five generations and two continents." Tom Wigley's grandfather immigrated to Detroit in 1924 from Liverpool, England. With him he brought his family trade of meat processing, passed down through the generations from his great grandfather.

Over a century ago in Liverpool, Frank Wigley, Tom's grandfather cured corned beef in a brine solution in oak barrels. During this period, Frank developed a delicious flavor with a careful balance of selected spices. Today, Tom and Jim Klein, his partner for over twenty years, process their corned beef with the same formula in a scrupulously clean plant with state-of-the-art equipment on Hale Street at the northern edge of the Eastern Market area. The well-trimmed briskets are sealed in a special bag which can be used for cooking. Keeping it in this bag when you cook it gives a stronger, spicy flavor to the meat.

As Tom says, "we do such a fine job of curing the beef, you only need a pot of water to cook it in."

---

**Ronnie's Quality Meats**
**1445 E. Kirby**

---

Ronnie's Quality Meats occupied the east side of the main aisle of Gratiot Central Market in the late '60's, facing Wigley's Quality Meats on the west side of the aisle. "People had special feelings about that particular building, a fun place to go." One of the greatest episodes in its history was the Great Corned Beef War.

> Wigleys were primarily the corned beef people, I was the lamb man. They started selling lamb, so I started selling corned beef. Who was going to sell the corned beef cheaper? It was pennies; two cents cheaper, three cents cheaper, back and forth. On one Friday night's news program, a television reporter interviewed me. The news media wanted to make a real vendetta out of it. She asked, "Ron, how cheap will

you get?" and I said, "Well, I'll probably give it away free--I <u>will</u> give it away free." The next morning, Saturday about 7:00 a.m., customers were lined up across the bridge five deep. Business escalated.

This went on for three weeks, and we made every major newspaper and magazine in the country. Every radio station and newspaper in the country was calling. There were reporters everywhere, up and down the aisles in Gratiot Central, interviewing everybody. A major TV program spent the day with us. At that time, the price was down to twenty-nine cents a pound. That was the Corned Beef War of 1975. What fun!

The Bedways, of Lebanese descent, were the first to sell ready-to-broil shish-kabobs. Ron's son Tom, who has worked alongside his father since he was seven, is credited with the kabob idea. They grilled them at the Riverfront festivals, and today they still offer the kabobs at their retail store on Russell at Ferry and in the new Gratiot Central Market.

## Others

Germack's
1416 E. Fisher Freeway

Three generations of the Germack family have been importing pistachios to the U.S. from Turkey since 1924. American born, of Lebanese and Syrian descent, in the past they have maintained offices in New York and Detroit. Today the company headquarters and plant are located in Eastern Market on the Fisher Freeway Service Drive at Russell, where they process, package, and distribute dried nuts and fruits nationwide.

Germack was the first company to import pistachios from Turkey to the United States and also the first to color the pistachio shells red. In the old days, the nuts were dried on the ground after soaking the husks off the shells. Residue moisture caused the shells to discolor, an unappetizing mottled effect. Hence, red pistachios. Modern techniques make the dying unnecessary today, but a small percentage are still tinted.

Kitchen Et Cetera
2634 Orleans

Patrick Krekreghe (crake-CRAY-gee) thinks the Eastern Market provides the best venue for his product, a bean flour he calls "Beans 'R' Us." He markets his product to health food stores, restaurants, food service companies, and institutions like schools.

Patrick came to Detroit from Nigeria via New York City and the City University of New York. He and his wife and two children find Detroit a place of great opportunity and potential to see his business dreams come true.

The unique nature of Patrick's bean product is that it doesn't produce abdominal gas because he removes the hard-to-digest high-fiber hull. The bean, taken through his process, creates a high-protein bean flour.

In the Market, the flour is available at Hirt's and Rafal's.

# ⌘ Market Sheds ⌘

## 🚐 Vendor & 🚜 Farmer

Michigan, Ohio, and Canadian farmers have been the centerpiece and mainstay of Detroit's Eastern Market from its beginning on Cadillac Square. Many of them still come to Market six days a week. They are the focus of Saturday Market day.

Originally, the farmers occupied three sheds, running north from Vernor Highway between Russell and Market Streets. Construction of the Fisher Freeway, begun in 1965, changed the appearance of the Market. Vernor Highway was replaced by the Fisher Freeway. Eventually, Shed #1 was moved to Belle Isle and used to stable horses. Shed #1's space became a parking area and Vernor became the Fisher Freeway Service Drive. Today, we keep the old designations, therefore we have no Shed #1. The pedestrian bridge spanning the Freeway completed the project.

Besides the farmers highlighted in this section, we pay homage to a group of truck-farmers who come to the Market for the eight to ten peak weeks of the Michigan season. Mike Kielbasa, Shed #2, from Columbus, Michigan, still comes with his honey, perfect vegetables, and sometimes flowers as do Donald Everett, Clinton; the Benders from Southfield; Martin Schamm, Mt. Clemens; Louis Konowalski, Adrian; Norman Harms, Mt. Clemens. We apologize to those we've missed and look forward to your fine produce next year.

🚐 Tony Moceri and his wife, Glenda, of **Moceri and Sons**, operate the big, colorful stall on the southeast corner of Shed #2, a prime spot.  Their top grade produce and bushel sales make traffic heavy on any Saturday morning.

Tony Moceri learned the produce business from his Dad, coming to the Market every day at 4 a.m.  That was over fifty years ago.

🚐 Don Schneider, (Shed #2) a glass artisan from Plymouth, working in lampworked and blown glass, creates beads, marbles, cabochons, ornaments, paperweights, vases, bowls, knobs and more.  But on Saturdays, he operates the **Lux Produce** stall #201 in Shed #2, providing Market goers with a tantalizing variety of mushrooms (portobellos, cremini, lobsters), a good selection of in and out-of-season fruits, and fresh mixed baby greens (mesclun), all air-freighted overnight.  Schneider's father lends a helping hand on Saturdays.

Schneider suggests that you store mushrooms in a paper bag in the refrigerator when you get home from the Market.

> **Lux Produce** is named for my maternal grandfather, Morris Lux.  His mother started this stall after emigrating from Russia shortly after the turn of the century.  I am our fourth generation at the Eastern Market.  As a small child, I would stand on a wooden crate selling onions at twelve for $1.00.  My experience is lifelong, over thirty years of serious commitment.

🛒 Dorothy Barg, (Shed #2) from Lapeer, first came to Eastern Market as a young child with her father, who dressed poultry, made butter and sold eggs and extra produce from their gardens, primarily potatoes and root vegetables. Barg was "permitted" to help with sales when she learned to make change and to figure the price of a chicken by multiplying (in her head) the weight and the price per pound.

After she married, she and her husband continued raising produce to take to Eastern Market. Their Roma tomatoes were the best to be found. Later, when her husband retired from General Motors, they started a greenhouse. Herbs were having a revival, and one greenhouse soon grew to three, and **The Herb Garden** became a reality.

> I still love to 'play' in the dirt, and cannot abide Bingo, so I'm continuing the lifelong marriage tradition of coming to the Market that my husband and I enjoyed together. My daughter and son-in-law indulge my continuing joy in Eastern Market by helping me with their time and spirit.

**Lawrence Zienert** owns and runs a fifty-acre farm near Washington, Michigan. Located in the third stall on the right of Shed #2, he has been there rain or shine since 1927 selling his product, farm-fresh eggs. He also grows spinach, onions, greens, carrots, and tomatoes.

Zienert loves the Market and speaks fondly of his time spent there. He put all his children through college with his business, and you often meet one of them or one of his grandchildren on a Saturday. His story gives us a taste of another era.

# Market Sheds_____

I started coming to Market with my Dad in 1927. His first truck was a Model T with hard rubber tires on the rear.

In those days, Market started at 5 a.m. going until 9 p.m. Later, it changed to 8 p.m., then 6 p.m. Stall rent was $.25 a half day. Now [1998], it's $24.00 a half day. The cleaning crew was busy all day, going between trucks with push brooms and shovels picking up garbage. At the end of the day, the whole Market was hosed down and brushed by tractors.

The wing on our shed from the concessions to Russell sold live poultry on Saturday. The Market was solid with trucks side by side, and the aisle packed with people early. Many of the big stores, Dexter-Davison, Shire Brothers from Chene-Gratiot, A&P, Kroger, C.F. Smith, and Farmer Jack came early. On our way to Market, we passed a lot of vendors with push carts and one-horse-drawn wagons. At first, there were only three sheds, so many farmers sold along the curb as far out as where the old Detroit Correction House stood. Farmers from far away would come the night before. It was not unusual to see dozens of cots behind the trucks for them to sleep until Market opened.

Probably some of my most memorable times were during the Depression years.  If my Dad stopped for groceries on the way home after a full day and he had $3 left over, we felt we had a good day.  In 1933, we sold sweet corn five dozen in a bag, seven bags for $1, eggs $.12-$.18 a dozen.  Tomatoes sold four bushels for $1.00.  Egg cartons weren't even around then.  People brought their own baskets, or we put them in paper bags.

🚜 Sandra Sawicki (Shed #2), with her husband Joseph, owns and runs **J & S Sawicki Organic Produce and Flowers**.  Sandra had five years of agricultural study in Poland, equivalent to a Masters degree in Agriculture in the U.S. "Back in Poland I managed greenhouses, but I wanted to travel."

In 1978, she moved to Chicago to live with an aunt and she met and married Joseph.  They came to Michigan and farmed with Joseph's parents in Capac.  That's when they began going to the Eastern Market.  In 1989, they bought an eighty-acre farm near Imlay City.  Today, they sell organically grown carrots, green beans, sweet corn, broccoli, okra, tomatoes, peppers, Brussels sprouts, red beets, and spinach greens for the Fall season.

The Sawickis are located just inside Shed #2 on the right where Sandra creates personalized bouquets to order.  Every year, they grow more flowers for cut-flower arrangements.  The children, Steve, Andrea and Marek, pitch in taking orders, selling produce and their popular Amish popcorn.

🚜 **Shirley Jentzen** (Shed #2) owns a 28-acre farm in Monroe. She and her husband Jack have sold from the same Market stall for over 25 years. Shirley started with her mother and father who had a stall in the original Shed #1 in 1939 and has been at the Market virtually every Saturday since.

> I would sooner do this than work 9 to 5, five days a week. I love it down here. I love it. And I love putting seeds into the ground and watching them grow. Take that teeny, tiny seed and watch it turn into a great big plant.

Her parents started with produce, chickens and eggs. She continued the tradition of eggs, and added some produce like peppers, cucumbers, potatoes, carrots, tomatoes, and flowers. One of her specialties is herbs, fresh in season and dried in winter. Shirley creates beautiful sugared panoramic eggs for the Easter season.

Shirley's stall is enhanced by her trademark, a handmade quilt her mother pieced together over twenty years ago, covering one of her tables.

🚜 **Haack's Farm Produce** has been in the Market in the same stall since 1935 in Shed #2. June Haack points to four of the five generations working in the stall today. "I've worked here since I was five years old and so have my children and now my grandchildren. There is no better learning experience for a child than being in this Market." Their farm is in Columbus, MI., and one of their sons owns Haack's Farm and Greenhouses in Armada. They all proudly wear Haack's Farm Produce T-shirts in the summer, switching to their logo-decorated sweatshirts. Haacks grow a great variety of produce. Zucchini is a specialty.

June Haack also creates fall arrangements of their wheat. Customers look for their painted pumpkins in the fall.

🚜 **Alan Bzenko**, (Shed #2) from Rochester, sells honey. He started selling at Eastern Market in 1940. At that time, he had 400 hives; today, he has 150. He says, "Honey prices have gone up dramatically, from 50 cents for 5 lbs. to $7.75. There were seven of us beekeepers selling honey, now it is down to two."

Besides jars of the golden nectar, he carries honey candy. For something to light up a special meal, Bzenko makes and sells hand-rolled beeswax candles.

🚜 **Alfred and Helen Penzien** (Shed #2) come from Imlay City. The Penziens have been in the Market forever. They have a beautiful selection of vegetables, and their beets are a specialty.

🚐 Jerry Robbins (Shed #2) and his family are a familiar sight at his Eastern Market **Dorn-Robbins** stall #281-283. Oak Park residents, Jerry and his daughter provide some of the best fresh garlic in the Market and other good seasonal produce. Listen for his cry, "Buy your birth-control pills here."

Robbins has a 1920's picture of the Eastern Market on display at his stall. His family, originally Robinowitz, have been around the Market for four generations. Jerry, retired now from his family firm of Dorn Fruit and Produce, continues to sell retail in the same stall he and his family have used since 1934. He proclaims, "four generations and still moving forward."

🛒 **Ann Bondy Farms** (Shed #2) has been at the Market since the days when they brought their produce by horse and cart, and took the ferry across the Detroit River from Canada. Ann Bondy and her husband met at the Market. Ann, née Bidoul and of Belgian decent, grew up on a farm in Roseville, Michigan. She was the oldest of nine. Her French husband was the youngest of nine, from River Canard, Canada, where Ann moved after her marriage. She found that Canadian farmers had an advantage at the Market because their produce was ready two weeks before U.S. farmers.

Simon, Ann's son, runs the farm and goes to the wholesale Market during the week as well as the Saturday Market. On Saturdays, they sell retail and wholesale at their stall, #294 . They start with bedding plants in April and switch to vegetables in Mid-June. Their specialties are home-grown fresh lettuces, parsley, herbs, carrots, beets, tomatoes, peppers, radishes, green onions, leeks, basil, cabbage, greens, turnips, spinach, melons. It is not unusual for them to have thirty different items on the table at one time.

The Odrobina sisters, Ann, Mary Ann, Pauline Ann, and Antoinette (Butch) have stalls in Sheds #3 and #4. As children, they came to the Market together to help their Dad. Today, one works the family farm in New Haven, and the other three have farms of their own. With their children, they help each other selling at the Saturday Market.

🛒 **Ann Odrobina**, the oldest, works with her husband, John Gaier, on Saturday year round. When the seasons change, so do their products.  From spring peas to summer corn, they switch to pork in the winter.

Thanksgiving to Easter, the Gaier's set up their refrigerated trucks in their stall in Shed #3, selling fresh pork.  "Tender, juicy pork meat comes from healthy, well-fed #1 hogs.  Look for pink meat and a good layer of fat," says Ann.

🚐 **John D. Hill** (Stall #377, Shed #3) grew up in the Keweenaw Peninsula at the northern-most tip of Michigan's Upper Peninsula in the early '60's, and moved to Sandusky, Ohio, after serving a stint in the Army in Korea. "In the later 1960's, I began selling produce in the Eastern Market and in other smaller seasonal markets.  The Market has been good over the years.  I meet a lot of nice people and I always try to provide what the customers want--quality produce, at a fair price."

🚐 **Lucille (Willis) Coles**, (Shed #3) in the Market since 1968, is known as the "Green Bean Lady."  She says, "I love people and my customers love me.  I have a senior citizen couple who have been coming for twenty years.  One week I couldn't get good beans and I told them another dealer had better and cheaper beans than mine.  They said they wanted mine."

🚜 **Henry Turman**, in Shed #3, a farmer from Fitchfield says, "I farm and specialize in the produce I grow on the farm.  I've been at the Market since 1957 and am very glad to have a few weeks out of the year to serve people that like to get good vegetables, home grown." People line up for Turman's fresh lima beans in the Fall.

🚐 Armand Lombardi (Shed #3) has been working at the Market since he was a boy in the early 1940's, when vegetables sold for twenty-five cents a basket.  As a kid, he had to buy a badge for a dollar to sell his wares.  The Market master rang a bell at 5:00 a.m., signaling that farmers could start selling.  Today, Lombardi helps his son, who owns **G and M Produce**, sell fruits and vegetables on Saturday in their Shed #2 stall.

🚜 **Carncross Sugar Bush** in Clare, MI., has had a Market stall since 1984 (Shed #4 in Summer, #3 in Winter), but they've been making maple syrup since the late 1800's when Lawrence Carncross' grandfather came from upstate New York and purchased the farm.  Today, Lawrence and his father, Everett, continue that tradition, and perhaps one day his young daughter will as well.  Lawrence, with a degree in agriculture from Michigan State, decided to "live off the land."  He modernized the production of syrup, and what started out as a few gallons burgeoned into a business of 100,000 gallons a year.

The maple syrup season is short, from the first of March to the middle of April.  The weather must be perfect for the sap to run--45 degrees during the day and 22-25 degrees at night.  Once a tree buds, the season is over.  It takes 40 gallons of sap to make one gallon of syrup.  There are over 7,000 taps in the Carncross maples, often more than one per tree.  Carncross offers three grades of syrup: Grade A, a lighter syrup, medium amber in color with a delicate flavor;  Grade B, darker with a stronger flavor like sorghum; and Grade C, the darkest and strongest of all.

Carncross sells in many regional farm markets and Eastern Market every Saturday.  Rafal's Spice Company carries their product and Russell Street Deli serves it with their pancakes.

# ⊂ℜ *Market Shoppers* ℬ

## *Saturday*

     Saturday at Eastern Market is a happening, a family tradition for hundreds of shoppers, filling their carts and bags with good local produce, fine meats and cheeses, and whetting their appetites for the week to come. Price haggling, people watching, and picking out the most creative shopping carts compete for the number-one sport. Homemade shopping bags, fancy new carts, or the kids' old rusty-red Radio Flyer--anything to haul away the great bargains.

     The most serious of the average 15,000 Saturday customers arrive early to get the freshest pick. In the busiest summer weeks, many sellers are set up by 6 a.m., some even earlier. Bargins begin by early afternoon. Much later, the pungent perfumes of overripe peaches, melons, and tomatoes fill the air. Wholesale distributors with stalls in the sheds lower their prices on produce that won't keep over the weekend.

     Market-area restaurants do a brisk business. Meeting friends for Saturday breakfast or lunch is a tradition with many Market shoppers who never mind the long lines. Good carry-out foods are available, too.

     Saturday Market customers reflect the diversity of the Metro Detroit area.

     **Leonard Leone**, retired Wayne State University professor, feels that Eastern Market played a significant role in his young life.

> My association with Eastern Market began
> in 1929 when my father established Leone

Imported Foods, specializing in Italian foods. I worked with my father on weekends and summers while attending high school and college. I have fond memories of the colorful and busy market place where merchants spoke many languages selling their products. In our store, one was always greeted by the enticing aromas of imported cheeses, salamis and the visual delight of a wide range of pastas, olives and canned goods from many countries. After my father's retirement in 1940, the business was continued by his brother, Nunzio Leone and his sons.

**Dulcie Rosenfeld** shops the Market and expresses her feeling this way: "I have been taking pictures of produce for twenty years of Eastern Marketing--and plenty of Flower Days, too. It's marvelous to report that the color photos of the 70's look exactly like the ones taken in recent months. Only the photograpopher and some of the marketers have aged. Otherwise, the Market is always fresh."

**Louise (Lou) Flaviani Scott** has fond memories of weekly trips with her father to Eastern Market.

It was a delight driving down Gratiot Avenue in Papa's shiny black '37 Ford. I was awed by the host of people, the amount of fruits, cheeses, meats, poultry. As a reward for our weekly trek, I was blessed with the best Italian meals imaginable.

Even folks who have moved away from Detroit still recall their times spent at the Market. A resident of London, Ontario, **Carol Agocs** lived in Detroit for many years, giving friends and family home-made, nutritious foods created from her Eastern Market trips.

> I remember taking the kids to Eastern Market when they were small, and how fascinated they were with the profusion of colors and shapes of the vegetables and fruits piled high, and the busy people who always had time to grin at a child.

The Hunger Action Coalition, a group of citizens dedicated to abolishing hunger in Michigan, provides public education, public policy monitoring and advocacy, and coordinates hunger relief efforts. **Nida Donar**, executive director of the Coalition, lives two blocks from Eastern Market. "We come to the Market late in the day and walk around to catch the good deals."

As a fund raiser, HAC publishes a cookbook, <u>The More The Merrier</u>, full of recipes to feed a crowd. "Soup makers living in Detroit have a great advantage because of our wonderful year-round Eastern Market."

**Judy Jagenow**, the retail store manager of R. Hirt Jr., recalls a story her father, Walter J. Campau, born in 1918, told about her grandfather.

> Grandpa used to come to Eastern Market as a young man from the family farm in Mt. Clemens, not far from my home in Clinton Township. He used Gratiot Avenue to get to

the Market as I do today, going to work at R. Hirt. There were, however, several differences between his trips a hundred years ago and mine today. What takes me about thirty-five minutes took Grandpa two to three days. The reason for this big difference? The road I travel today is well-paved with cement and asphalt and an occasional pothole. Back then, Grandpa suffered a corduroy dirt road. And while I drive a Thunderbird to the Market, Grandpa Campau was driving a herd of cattle. Often, when stranded in a traffic jam, I calm myself by realizing that the driving conditions could be worse and a hundred years ago, they were.

Several professional artists have their studios in and around the Market and find it a great place for motivating the illusive spirit of creativity.

Professional photographer **Michelle Andonian** lives and works in her renovated studio in Rocky's Lofts over the Johnny Mack Bakery.

I've been a big Market fan all my life. I grew up in Southwest Detroit. When we were little kids, my Mom always brought us to the Rocky Peanut Company which was in this building at that time. Before the big Fourth of July Fireworks in downtown Detroit, she would buy a twenty-five pound bag of peanuts and we would bag them up in

little brown paper sacks and sell them for a
quarter at the fireworks. I find it
especially ironic that I am running my
business out of the very building that we
came to as children to learn how to be in
business.

The artist in her believes that Eastern Market
should not be rebuilt or redesigned. "It is what it is. You
have to preserve what is naturally here." She has been in
the Market for over ten years, photographing it in all
seasons.

So many interesting people. There's the egg
man--what a beautiful face he has. It's
funny, but I always call the people by what
they are, like the honey man, the egg man.
Everyone gets those nicknames after awhile.
David Hirt is the cheese guy, and now they
call me the photographer lady.

"I get a sense of freedom and security at the
Market. It's one of the three places I'm at home: the
Market, the campus, and the broadcast studio." From an
early age, eight or nine, to this day, the Market has been a
place of learning and living for **Saul Wineman**. As a very
young boy, he remembers going to the Market on days when
his father wasn't working, like Jewish holidays, just running
an errand or listening to his father "rapping in Yiddish."
Albert Wineman was a kind but distant father, quiet and
reserved at home. But in the Market, he was a public
person. The Market was his place, his stage, talking to his

customers and other businessmen, talking about serious things with his son. By the time Saul was thirteen, he worked every Saturday with his father, making the rounds as "the jumper" on the truck, delivering smoked fish to the customers who, like Albert, were all Eastern European immigrant Jews. "We'd load up the truck at the plant, General Smoked Fish (they were processors) on Winder Street. I'd go through a whole day not hearing English, only Yiddish."

To Detroit radio and television audiences, Saul Wineman is known as Paul Winter. Back in the early 1950's, he had an early morning show on WXYZ. After the show, he'd often stop at the Market to see his father, knowing he'd be at Samuel Brothers Cafeteria until 7:30 every morning. Samuel Brothers was his hangout for years. A big cafeteria with tables on either side of the food line, it was "like a New York deli."

"As I grew older, my Market going was intermittent until we came home from Boston in 1965 and my father was very ill and I started going regularly every Saturday. After my father died in 1973, it was a ritual. It became my *kaddish*, a sacred thing to do." Saul would "take a stroll," stopping to talk to all the people who had known his father, like the "egg lady" in Shed #3 or the flower grower whose father and grandfather had been in the Market for over sixty-five years. When he had a show on WJR, he'd often tell his listeners he'd "see you at the Market."

## Weekday

Watching the Market at work during the week when it primarily transacts wholesale business is exciting, but you have to get there early. The Market day begins around 2 a.m. when local traffic gives way to delivery vans, refrigerated semis and flatbed trucks that jam the narrow streets. Fork-lifts and hand trucks scurry about, loading foodstuffs bound for local grocers and restaurants. By noon, the trucks have gone and business winds down around 2 p.m., except for the surrounding retail shops, which close at 4 p.m.

One can shop the Market during the week and never set foot in a supermarket. For basic foods, try Capital Poultry's milk and buttermilk besides their poultry and fish. In addition to their cheeses, Hirt's carries fresh eggs and butter, phyllo pastry, and deli meats. For bread: Johnnie Mack's Bakery or the Bagel Factory. Gabriel Importing stocks a complete selection of fresh Middle Eastern breads. (They also sell odd-lots of soaps, like laundry soaps and cakes of olive oil soap for the bath.) Hirt's sells fine European breads from Chamberlain Bakery, Avalon Bakery, and Deli Unique.

Coffees, teas, and bottled beverages are found at Rafal's, Rocky's, and Hirt's. Each carries many choices of sodas, fruit juices, sparkling waters. Of course, Tim's Cost Plus Wines awaits if you want something more festive.

Fresh meats are available at the custom-cut meat counter at Wigley's in Royal Diamond, up the street on Russell, or at Gratiot Central Market. They also have a good selection of processed meats, as does Rocky Peanut.

Palazzolo and Ciaramitaro sell retail fruits and vegetables at the entrances to their warehouses during the week.

You can find just about everything at the Market, even supermarket stuff like pet food, paper goods, and cleaning supplies. If you're tired of artificial lights and Muzak, this is a good alternative.

Businesses on Gratiot add other products to Market shopping. A fun place to browse is Cheap Charley's next to Capital Poultry. Charley has great bargains on dishes, often stacks of surplus, army-regulation china for $1 a piece and he sells an inexpensive grocery cart, great for Market going.

Busy Bee Hardware, at the corner of Gratiot and Russell, has stacks of pots and pans, bins of screws and nails, and piles of paints and brushes. If you need keys made or a new lock, Mikey's Lock and Key, located in Busy Bee, can do it. Founded in 1918, Busy Bee still sells Ferry garden seeds as they did then, when farmers used Busy Bee as their seed source. Seeds are still stored in the original glass jars.

On the other side of Gratiot, loft apartments and art studios have been created within the old Atlas Furniture Mart. At the corner of Russell and Gratiot is Fuch's Candle Store, established in 1891. It "has served spiritual needs for over a hundred years," selling candles, oils, stones, incense, herbs, soaps, and religious articles. At Fuchs "old traditions and new-age beliefs come together." They also stock Dr. Bronner's Pure-Castile Soap. A few drops diluted in water cleans your fruits and vegetables.

The Eastern Market area fills many daily-living needs, as area residents will tell you. It may not do it all, but it's a pleasant way to shop.

Gordes
10 FOR $1

# ɔ꒰ Market Recipes ꒱ɞ

The recipes that follow reflect the foods sold at Eastern Market.  Some are quite simple with only two or three ingredients (Spinach/Strawberry Salad, Green Beans with Smoked Turkey Wings,) and others more complex (Pizza Rustica, Minestrone with Kale).  Some come from family recipe files over fifty years old (Refrigerator Pickles, Sour-Cream Twists), others follow newer trends in cooking (Cajun Pumpkin Bisque with Shrimp).  None of them rely on canned soups or prepared mixes.  Rather, they emphasize fresh market produce, dairy products, and meats.  All ingredients for these recipes can be purchased at Eastern Market.

Recipes were contributed by Market customers, employees, dealers, farmers, restaurant and store owners, and vendors.  All have been tested by the authors.  Any significant changes are marked "*" and explained as *Editor's Notes.  All measurements are level unless otherwise noted and all oven temperatures are pre-heated.

# Warm Roquefort/Bacon Spread

This crowd pleaser was perfected by
Market shopper Abby Kercorian.

8 slices lean smoked bacon, diced
2 cloves garlic, minced
8 ounces Pauli cream cheese
4 ounces Roquefort cheese
1/4 cup light cream
2 Tbs chives
3 Tbs smoked almonds, chopped

○    In non-stick skillet, slowly cook bacon
to render all fat.  Drain bacon on paper towel and
discard fat.  Sauté garlic in skillet until soft and
stir in cheeses, cream, chives, and bacon.  Mix
gently but thoroughly with wooden spoon.  Spoon
mixture into oiled 2-cup baking dish.
○    Sprinkle with chopped almonds and
bake, lightly covered with foil, 30 minutes in a
pre-heated 350° oven.  Serve with sliced baguette,
crackers, or vegetables.  Makes 1 2/3 cups.

# Shangleesh Appetizer

Instructions from Gabriel Import (p. 25) for serving their famous yogurt cheese.

○ *Place the ball of Shangleesh in the center of a large platter. You can leave it whole or break it into pieces. Surround it with a ring of chopped tomatoes, onions, and cucumbers. Drizzle generously with imported virgin olive oil, and serve with fresh pita bread.*

Editor's note:
to serve Shangleesh as a salad, first cover the platter with a layer of shredded Romaine lettuce tossed with a light vinaigrette then top with the crumpled cheese and chopped vegetables.

# Artichoke Dip

All of the ingredients for Judy Jagenow's (p. 61) Dip can be found at Hirts.

> 1 14-ounce can artichokes in water, drained
> 1 cup Parmesan cheese, grated
> 1/2 lb Monterey Jack cheese, shredded
> 1 cup mayonnaise

○ Chop and blend all ingredients together. Put in a greased 1-qt casserole and bake uncovered at 350° for 1/2 hour until it bubbles. Serve with crackers, cocktail breads, or tortilla chips.

# Baked Mushrooms

*Cremini or white medium-size mushrooms*
        *(allow 4-6 per person)*
*Juice of 1 lemon*
*Pesto (store-bought or Pesto with Roasted*
        *Garlic, p. 94)*
*Grated Parmesan cheese*

O *Clean mushrooms with damp paper toweling and remove stems (save for a soup). Rinse mushrooms in lemon juice and drain well. Fill cavities with pesto and top each mushroom with 1 Tbs cheese. Arrange in an oven-going shallow dish (crumpled foil in the dish will keep them from sliding around), and bake in a pre-heated 425° oven 13-15 minutes. Place on a napkin-covered serving plate.*

# Champagne Punch

Jim McCarthy, owner of Cost Plus Wines (p. 23), serves his champagne punch at festive family occasions.

*3 liters Chablis*
*2 bottles of inexpensive champagne*
*1/2 bottle of Guinness stout*
*1 quart sweet cherries*
*Citrus fruit*

○ *Freeze washed cherries individually in water-filled ice cube trays. Combine Chablis, champagne, and stout. Float cherry ice cubes and slices of fresh citrus fruits to flavor and garnish the punch.*

Notes:

# Spiced Cider

𝒜 steaming pot of spiced cider for a winter welcome.

*Bring to a simmer in large kettle:*
*2 quarts fresh apple cider*
*Juice of 1/2 lemon*
*1/3 cup brown sugar*
*2 bay leaves*
*2 cinnamon sticks*
*3 whole cloves*
*1/2 tsp cardamom*
*1/2 tsp freshly grated nutmeg*
*Peel of one well-scrubbed orange*

○ *Simmer 30 minutes, strain, and keep warm to serve.*

# White Sangria

This variation of traditional Sangria is lighter in alcohol, delicious for a wedding shower or summer party.

1 each peach, nectarine, and plum,
 peeled and thinly sliced
1 orange, washed, sliced, and seeded
1/2 lemon washed, sliced, and
 seeded
1 cup white grapes, washed
12 mint leaves, washed and dried
1 bottle fruity white wine
2 cups sweetened lemonade
1/2 cup orange liquor

O Mix together in large pitcher and refrigerate overnight. Serve chilled, garnished with fresh fruit.

# Cajun Pumpkin Bisque with Shrimp

As an elegant beginning for a festive holiday dinner, this soup is a conversation piece.  The vegetable base is flavorful without the shrimp and freezes well.

*1 Tbs butter*
*1 small onion, chopped*
*2 medium leeks, white part only,*
*        well-washed and thinly sliced*
*4 cloves garlic, minced*
*2 stalks celery, peeled and sliced*
*1 medium potato, diced*
*2 cups peeled, chopped pumpkin or*
*        unsweetened canned pumpkin*
*2 medium tomatoes, peeled, seeded, and*
*        chopped*
*6 cups chicken or vegetable stock*
*2 tsp salt, or to taste*
*1 Tbs salt-free Cajun seasoning (Rafal's*
*        brand preferred)*
*1/2 cup chopped Italian parsley*
*1/2 lb  peeled raw shrimp*
*2 cups light cream*
*Minced parsley and chives for garnish*

○  In large kettle (6 quart) gently cook onions, leeks, garlic, and celery in butter until soft. Add rest of vegetables, parsley, and stock.  Season with salt and Cajun spice and cook, covered, over gentle heat 30 minutes.  Cool slightly.

O  Process to purée or put in blender for a finer texture.

O  At serving time, put shrimp in blender with 1/2 cup soup and purée.  Reheat soup with shrimp purée and simmer over low heat for 10 minutes.  Gradually stir in cream and adjust seasoning.

O  Serve with a drizzle of cream and snipped herbs for garnish, or sauté a few extra shrimp to garnish.  Makes 2 quarts.

_Notes:_

# Eastern Market Soup

Nida Donar (p. 61) says her secret for good vegetable soup is sautéeing each vegetable before simmering them together in the vegetable stock.

2 cups shredded cabbage
4 large carrots, sliced
4 cups chopped celery with leaves
4 cups chopped onions
1/4 cup oil
1 gallon water
2 Tbs salt
12 peppercorns
2 bay leaves
6 large carrots
4 medium zucchini
4 medium yellow squash
8 green onions
4 ribs celery
1 Tbs oil or margarine
4 cups cooked beans
2 cups sliced cherry tomatoes
1 10 ounce can tomato sauce
8 ears corn*
1 tsp hot sauce

○ In a large stockpot, sauté the cabbage, carrots, celery, and onion in the oil for 5 to 8 minutes. Add water, salt, peppercorns, and bay *leaves. Bring to boiling; simmer for about 1 hour, or until the broth is well flavored. Strain the broth into a large glass bowl; the vegetable stock is ready to use (or it may be frozen for future use). Discard the cooked vegetables.*

*○ Pour broth into stockpot; bring to a boil. Slice the rest of the carrots diagonally; cut zucchini and yellow squash, green onions, and ribs of celery into thin slices. Sauté in 1 Tbs of oil. Add vegetables to boiling broth. Lower heat and simmer 15 minutes. Add cooked beans, cherry tomatoes, tomato sauce, corn, and hot sauce. Simmer 15 minutes and serve. Serves 25.*

*Editor's note:
In an open market buy corn that is protected from the sun.

**Nida Donar** is the Executive Director of the Hunger Action Coalition. The profits from the group's cookbook, The More The Merrier, go to feed the hungry. This is Donar's recipe as it appears in the book. She says to substitute whatever vegetables are available in the Market for this soup.

Donar lives two blocks from Eastern Market. "We come to the Market late in the day and just walk around and catch the good deals."

# Minestrone with Kale

Autumn is soup season. This rich minestrone takes time but is well worth the effort.

8 ounces dried Great Northern beans
8 ounces dried chick peas (garbanzos)
4-6 carrots, washed, peeled and diced, 1/2"
       dice
2 large onions, red or white, diced
3 large stalks celery, peeled and diced
4 cloves garlic, minced
1/2 cup extra-virgin olive oil
1 pint fresh tomatoes, peeled and chopped,
       or 1 pint tomato sauce
6-8 cups chicken or vegetable stock, or
       equivalent soup base diluted
       (available at R. Hirt Jr. Company)
Rind from Parmesan-Reggiano cheese*
4 firm zucchini, well-washed and cubed
1 bunch kale, well-washed and chopped**
1/2 cup dry white wine
1/2 cup white rice, preferably Arborio
1/2 cup minced Italian parsley
1/2 cup chopped fresh basil
Salt and freshly ground black pepper,
       to taste

○ Soak the beans separately, each in warm water to cover, overnight. In a heavy covered saucepan, cook the Great Northerns in fresh water to cover by 2" until tender, 1 1/2 to 2 hours, depending on age of beans. Cool slightly and purée in blender. Season with a little salt and set aside. Cook chick peas in same manner, keeping water level even with depth of beans, until barely tender, then let sit with cover askew for 2 hours. This can be done the day before and refrigerated.

○ In heavy soup pot, heat olive oil and sauté onions, carrots, celery, and garlic, stirring often until tender. Add tomatoes or sauce, puréed beans, chick peas with their cooking water, stock, and cheese rinds. Simmer, partially covered, 1 hour or until flavors are well integrated, stirring from time to time. Add zucchini and kale and continue simmering until kale is tender, about 1 hour. Add wine and rice. If soup seems too thick at this point, add a cup or two of water. Cook 20 minutes until rice is tender. When soup has cooked to your satisfaction, remove from heat. Stir in minced parsley and basil and check seasoning.

Makes 4-5 quarts.

Editor's note: When re-heating soups it is best to do only the amount for one meal, rather than re-heating the whole pot, which can deplete much of its nutritional value and make flavors mushy. Cool completely before freezing.

*Editor's note: R. Hirt sells Italian Parmesan-Reggiano as well as other imported Parmesan cheeses. Freeze the rinds for the day you want to make a special soup. They add great character to this minestrone.

**Editor's note: Wash crinkly greens like kale in warm water to relax their curl and release their dirt.

# Pasta e Fagioli

Laura Bommarito, soup chef at Russell Street Deli
(p. 29), prepares her version of this classic.

1 1/2 cups dried navy, kidney, or garbanzo
     beans, washed and soaked overnight
     in enough water to cover them plus 2"
3 whole cloves garlic
3 Tbs olive oil
5 cloves garlic, minced
2 red onions, chopped
3 stalks celery, chopped
2 carrots, chopped
1 tsp fresh rosemary, minced, or
     1/2 tsp dried rosemary, crushed
1/2 tsp dried oregano
1/2 tsp crushed red pepper flakes
Salt and freshly ground pepper
10 sun-dried tomatoes, chopped
3 plum tomatoes, chopped
1 bunch rapini, chopped (about 2 cups), or
     fresh spinach or frozen spinach
     (10oz. pkg.)
8 cups chicken broth
2 Tbs fresh parsley, minced
1 Tbs fresh basil, minced
1/2 lb small shells, elbow macaroni, orzo, or
     any small pasta shape

Parmesan or Romano cheese for garnish

O  Drain the beans, put in a large pot with enough water to cover.  Add the whole garlic cloves. (Salt also may be added.) Bring to a boil, reduce the heat, and simmer 1 1/2 hours or until tender. (Garbanzo beans may take longer.)
O  Meanwhile, sauté the minced garlic, onions, celery, and carrots in the olive oil for 10 minutes, or until the vegetables are almost soft. Now, add them to the soup pot with the beans.  Add salt and pepper, the sun-dried and plum tomatoes, rapini (or spinach) and the chicken broth. (Vegetable broth may be substituted.)
O  Bring to a boil again, reduce the heat, and simmer until the greens are done, about 15 minutes.
O  Meanwhile, cook pasta until al dente (firm to the bite), then add to the soup with the fresh parsley and basil.  Stir well and season to taste.  The consistency of this soup should be thick and hearty; almost a stew.  Garnish with a generous amount of grated Romano or Parmesan sprinkled on top of each serving.  Serves 6.

# Turkey Chili

John Vivio, owner and chef of Vivio's (p. 32), serves this chili, popular with the lunch crowd.

*2 cloves garlic*
*1 cup carrots, diced*
*1 cup celery, diced*
*1 cup onions, diced*
*1 cup bell pepper, diced*
*3 whole bay leaves*
*4 Jalapeño peppers or crushed red peppers*
*1 26-ounce can tomatoes, diced*
*3 or 4 cups raw turkey, diced\**
*2 or 3 Tbs chili powder*
*2 26-ounce cans kidney beans*
*1/4 cup olive oil*
*Salt and pepper to taste*

○ *Sauté the garlic and onions in the olive oil for 10 minutes, but do not brown. Add the carrots, celery, and bell peppers and sauté for 5 minutes. Add the jalapeño peppers or red pepper, diced tomatoes, and bay leaves. Add water for a thinner consistency. Allow the mixture to simmer for 5 minutes before adding the chili powder, turkey, beans, salt and pepper. Simmer for 1/2 hour.*

\*Editor's note: If you prefer to use ground turkey, sauté it after garlic and onions.

# Coleslaw Made Easy

Melinda Pacha remembers coming to the Market during her college days when time and money were short to make this zesty slaw.

*Coleslaw:*
*6 cups shredded cabbage*
*1 or more Red Delicious apples, unpeeled,*
*        cored, cubed, or grated*
*1/2 cup Blue cheese, crumbled*

*Dressing:*
*1/2 cup mayonnaise*
*1/2 cup plain yogurt*

○   *In a large bowl place cabbage, apple, and cheese. In a smaller bowl mix mayonnaise and yogurt. If you like it sweet, add some honey. Pour the dressing over the cabbage and mix well. Serves 6-8.*

**Melinda Pacha**, recalls one Summer soirée that included a roasted suckling pig and a delightful salad of cabbage, apples and blue cheese. "Everything we ate and drank that day came from Eastern Market, the original in one-stop-shopping."

# Refrigerator Pickles

This makes a fine addition to a meal of home-grown mid-west vegetables or to top your favorite burger. They go especially well with corn-on-the-cob.

*7 cups sliced cucumbers, unpeeled and thinly sliced (smaller cucumbers are best)*
*1 cup thinly sliced onion*
*1 cup thinly sliced red or green pepper (red is best)*
*1 tsp tumeric*
*1 tsp celery seed*
*1 tsp mustard seed*
*1 Tbs salt*
*2 cups sugar*
*1 cup cider or white wine vinegar*

○ *Mix vegetables and seasonings well in a large bowl. Stir sugar and vinegar to dissolve sugar, then pour over vegetables and mix thoroughly. Put in a glass jar or stone crock, cover well, and refrigerate for 3-5 days before serving. Stir gently each day.*

**Anne Hruska Parsons**, former Detroit resident and Eastern Market-goer, has happy memories of her Czech family's dinner table in Nebraska. She still makes her Aunt Carrie's pickles from the original hand-written recipe, over fifty years old.

# Tabbooleh

Enjoy this healthy Syrian-Lebanese delicacy as an appetizer or salad, depending on your menu.

*1 cup cracked wheat, fine*
*1 bunch green onions*
*2 large bunches parsley*
*1/2 bunch mint (optional)*
*4 large tomatoes*
*Juice of 4 lemons*
*1/2 cup olive oil*
*Salt and pepper to taste*

◯ *Soak wheat in water a few minutes. Squeeze dry by pressing between palms. Finely chop onions, parsley, mint leaves, and tomatoes. Add wheat, lemon juice, olive oil, salt and pepper. Mix well.*
◯ *Serve with fresh lettuce leaves, grape leaves, or Syrian bread used as scoops. Serves 6.*

> **Edward Deeb**, a staunch supporter of Eastern Market, serves as board chairman of EMMA (Eastern Market Merchants Association). Deeb conducts Detroit Historical Society Eastern Market tours. Join the group--it's well worth the time. He makes his own parsley salad.

# Spinach/Strawberry Salad

*A* vibrant salad for a July 4th picnic.

*Salad:*
*8 cups baby spinach leaves*
*2 cups strawberries, sliced*

*Vinaigrette:*
*2 Tbs dark balsamic vinegar*
*6 Tbs extra-virgin olive oil*
*Salt and pepper*

○ *Carefully wash and dry small, tender spinach leaves. Wash and hull fully ripe, medium sized berries and slice vertically in half or thirds.*
○ *Mix vinaigrette ingredients. Toss the spinach thoroughly with the dressing and then gently fold in the sliced berries. Serves 6.*

# Tomato and Red Onion Salad

Glenda Moceri (p. 49) makes this salad when tomatoes are at their peak, August and September. Her favorite part is the juice generated by the oil and water--great for dipping with hunks of crusty Italian bread.

> *2 large red onions*
> *4 or 5 large tomatoes*
> *1/2 cup olive oil*
> *1 1/2 cups water*
> *1/2 cup basil, fresh or dried*
> *Pepper to taste*

○ *Slice onions and tomatoes. Put in 1 1/2 quart dish. Add olive oil, water, basil and pepper. Mix and marinate for 1 hour.*

Notes:

# Melonball Compôte

This fruit salad uses watermelon and other excellent Michigan melons, a perfect warm summer evening dessert.

*1 cantaloupe*
*1 honeydew*
*1/2 watermelon*
*1 cup fresh blueberries*
*2/3 cup sugar*
*1/3 cup water*
*1 tsp lime rind, grated*
*6 Tbs lime juice*
*1/2 cup light rum*

○ *Prepare melons with melon baller, or cut into bite size pieces. Boil sugar and water for 5 minutes over medium heat. Add lime rind and let cool to room temperature. Stir in lime juice and rum. Pour over melons and berries. Chill. Serves 6-8.*

# Wild Rice Salad

Wild rice, native only to North America, rich in flavor and nutrition, can be found at Rocky's, Hirt's, and Rafal's.

> 1 1/2 cups wild rice, rinsed well and drained
> 8 cups water
> 1 1/2 tsp salt
> 2 carrots, cut in 1/4" dice
> 1 shallot, minced and squeezed dry in a towel
> 1 tsp Dijon mustard
> 1 Tbs dark Balsamic vinegar
> 3 Tbs walnut oil (or part olive oil)
> 1/2 cup toasted walnuts, cooled
> 1/4 cup Roquefort cheese, crumbled

○ Cook rice in simmering salted water, covered, for 45 minutes. Add carrots and cook 10 minutes longer. Drain well and cool in large mixing bowl. Add shallot. Make a vinaigrette with mustard, vinegar, and oil. Toss rice gently but thoroughly with vinaigrette. Refrigerate.

○ Bring to room temperature 1/2 hour before serving, stir in nuts. Garnish with crumbled Roquefort cheese. Serves 6-8.

# Basil Pesto with Roasted Garlic

Make and freeze in late summer when basil is available in large bunches and the season's new garlic is in.

2 cups fresh basil leaves, washed and patted dry
1/2 cup extra-virgin olive oil
2 Tbs pine nuts
1/2 tsp salt
6 cloves Roasted Garlic (p. 127)
3 Tbs soft butter
1/2+ cup grated Parmesan-Reggiano

○ Mix all in blender until smooth.
○ Makes 1 cup pesto, enough for 12-16 ounces of pasta.

Pesto freezes well, a joyous addition to winter menus. It will taste creamier if you add the butter and cheese after defrosting, but the fresh taste of basil will come through if you freeze with the cheese and butter mixed in.

Editors note: A spoonful of pesto adds zest to a bowl of minestrone or any vegetable soup.

# Opal Basil Vinegar

Enjoy Dorothy Barg's (p. 50) special vinegar in a dressing for salad greens.

*1/2 cup fresh opal basil leaves\**
*1 quart white wine vinegar*

○ *Pour warmed vinegar over coarsely chopped basil leaves in clean glass jar. Cover. Put in a dark, cool place for three weeks. Strain through cheesecloth.*

\*Editor's note:
Basil is best before it flowers. After it flowers, pinch out any buds or flowers to keep the leaves from tasting bitter.

# Orange/Lemon Thyme Vinegar

Alan Reid, Market customer, prepares this intriguing flavored vinegar.

> 1 quart white wine or champagne vinegar, heated to just below the boiling point
> 1 orange, zested (Grate off just the orange rind but no white pith. Always scrub citrus fruit well before grating.)
> 1/2-1 cup lemon thyme sprigs
> 2 bay leaves
> 12-15 whole cloves

○ Infuse all ingredients together for 2 months. Strain and pour into sterilized bottles, adding fresh sprigs of thyme and strips of orange peel. Keeps indefinitely at room temperature.

Notes:

# Spicy Tomatoes

2 shallots, minced
3-4 cloves garlic, minced
1/2 cup olive oil
6 Roma tomatoes (about 2 lbs) chopped,
        seeded, but not peeled
1 tsp fresh basil
2 tsp Tabasco*
Salt
Pepper
A pinch or two of sugar

○ Sauté shallots and garlic in olive oil. Add the remaining ingredients. Cook about 15-20 minutes. Serve over pasta. Shrimp sautéed in olive oil, stir-fried vegetables, or sliced grilled chicken breast may be added to the tomatoes. Sprinkle with Parmesan cheese.

*Editor's note:
1 tsp gave a nice bite, 2 would be quite spicy.

When Roma tomatoes are in plentiful supply at the Market, customer **Paulette Groen** makes this quick and terrific sauce. She doesn't want to miss the good deals she gets for a bushel.

# Ginger Plum Sauce

Simple and delicious.

1 lb plums, halved and pitted
1/4 cup maple syrup
1 Tbs fresh ginger, finely minced
2 Tbs fresh lemon juice
2 tsp cornstarch

○ Cut each plum half into three wedges. Heat them with syrup and ginger in heavy sauce pan, stirring. Cook until plums release their juices, about 4 minutes. Mix lemon juice and cornstarch in small bowl. Add to plums, stirring until thickened, about 2 minutes. Serve warm over frozen yogurt, ice cream, pancakes, or waffles. Makes 2 cups.

Notes:

# Cajun Marinade

1/2 cup soy sauce
1/2 cup olive oil
1/4 cup sesame oil
1/4 cup lemon juice
4-5 Tbs Rafal's Hot "Salt Free" Cajun
        Seasoning
2 Tbs grated fresh ginger
2 tsp dry mustard
2 tsp Tabasco sauce

○ Combine all ingredients thoroughly.
○ This large amount will marinate 3 dozen large shrimp or 12-16 pieces of chicken. It really is HOT so don't marinate the meat for more than 30 minutes. For shrimp, thread on soaked wooden skewers (don't crowd the pieces) and grill for 2 minutes a side. For grilled chicken, turn pieces often and cook until juices run clear.

Notes:

# Cornbread Bean Pie
## (meatless)

From Bob Cerrito, chef/owner of Russell Street Deli (p. 29) and Flat Planet Pizza, a zesty supper dish in a southwest mode.

*Cornbread:*
*3 Tbs butter, melted*
*2 cups corn meal*
*3 Tbs flour*
*1 Tbs baking powder*
*1 Tbs sugar*
*1/2 tsp salt*
*1 3/4 cups milk*
*1 egg*

*Filling:*
*1 onion*
*1 green or sweet red pepper*
*1 cup dry beans or 2 cups canned (red,*
*        black, or any favorite bean)*
*1 to 2 tsp chili powder*
*Salt and pepper*
*1/2 cup or more cheddar or other*
*        cheese, shredded*
*Paprika for decoration*

○ If using dry beans, soak overnight. Rinse and change water; simmer until soft.

○ Preheat oven to 400°, and place 10" cast-iron skillet in oven while it is preheating.

○ Prepare filling: dice onion and pepper. Sauté in a few drops of oil or butter. Add chili powder and cooked, drained beans. Season to taste with salt and pepper. Continue cooking until heated through; remove from heat.

○ Prepare cornbread: mix dry ingredients in a bowl. Beat egg; add milk. Mix quickly into dry ingredients, then stir in melted butter.

○ To assemble: remove skillet from oven and butter it. Pour in 1/3 of the cornbread batter. Drop the bean mixture by spoonfuls onto the batter; cover with cheese and top with remaining batter. Decorate with slices of green or red pepper and sprinkle with paprika. Bake 25 minutes or until cooked through. Cut into wedges and serve hot with a great salsa on the side.

Notes:

# Spinach and Ricotta Cheese Crèpes
## (meat optional)

Lou Flaviani Scott (p. 60) passes on this fine family recipe.

*Classic Crèpes:*
*2 eggs*
*2 Tbs melted butter*
*1 1/3 cup milk*
*1 cup all purpose flour*
*1/2 tsp salt*

○ *Place ingredients in blender or food processor, cover and process for 20-30 seconds. Scrape down sides of container and process a few more seconds. If it thickens on standing, thin with a little milk. Batter should be thin enough to run freely around bottom of crèpe pan.*
○ *Heat a heavy non-stick 10"-12" skillet over medium heat until drop of water sputters on its surface. Lightly spray skillet with oil, stir batter with one hand, and with the other, tilt and rotate the pan as you pour in the batter, coating the bottom of the hot pan. Cook crèpe 60 seconds, flip over, and cook other side 45 seconds. Turn out onto cooling rack and continue until all batter is used, remembering to stir batter between each crèpe. As crèpes cool, stack them, separating each with a square of waxed paper. May be done up to two days in advance. Store in airtight bag and*

keep refrigerated. Makes 14-16 crèpes (6") or 18-22 crèpes (5").

*Spinach and Ricotta cheese filling:*
*1 package (10 oz.) frozen spinach,*
        *cooked and drained*
*1 Tbs butter*
*1/2 cup finely chopped onion*
*Dash dried red pepper flakes*
*1/2 tsp dried basil*
*1/2 tsp dried thyme*
*1 cup Ricotta cheese*
*1/3 cup grated Parmesan cheese*
*Salt and freshly ground pepper*
*Dash nutmeg*
*1/2 cup diced ham or prosciutto*

○ *Preheat oven to 375 °. Drain and squeeze spinach until dry as possible, chop coarsely. Melt butter in medium skillet. Sauté onion, red pepper flakes, basil and thyme for 5-6 minutes, until onion is soft, not brown. Add spinach and cook 1-2 minutes. Remove from heat and stir in Ricotta, Parmesan and remaining ingredients.*
○ *Fill and roll crèpes. Place in buttered ovenproof serving dish. Top with Cheese Sauce (see below), heat in oven about 10 minutes until lightly browned and bubbly.*

*Cheese sauce:*
*2 Tbs butter*
*2 Tbs flour*

1 1/4 cup milk
1/2 tsp Dijon mustard
1 tsp Worcestershire sauce
1/3 cup grated Parmesan cheese
Salt and white pepper

○ Melt butter in small saucepan over medium heat. Add flour and cook, stirring, for 2 minutes. Off heat, gradually blend in milk. Cook, stirring, until sauce thickens. Add mustard, Worcestershire sauce, cheese, salt and pepper. Heat through. Makes 1 1/2 cups.

*Notes:*

# Seasonal Vegetables with Polenta
## (meatless)

On Market day, pick a favorite combination of vegetables, clean and cut them into similar sizes and shapes, and toss together with a little olive oil (2 Tbs), a pinch of salt, a few grindings of pepper and a clove of garlic, minced. Let them sit for a half hour. Stir fry in a big wok or grill in a basket over hot coals (5-10 minutes) until tender. Toss with a handful of fresh herbs and spoon around mounds of warm polenta.

*Good vegetable possibilities:*
*Summer: Peppers (red, green, yellow), red onions, Portebello mushrooms, summer squash*
*Winter: broccoli (blanched 1 minute in boiling water), onions, and carrots (also blanched 1 minute), toss with Kalamata olives*
*Spring: asparagus, mushrooms, snow peas, and tomato flesh (added at last minute), with a sprinkling of grated lemon rind.*

O *Follow directions on polenta package, keeping polenta smooth and creamy. Turn polenta into individual pasta bowls or center on plates and surround with brightly colored vegetables. Pass lots of grated Parmesan or Asiago cheese.*

# Hirt Family Cheese Pie
## (meat optional)

Joyce DeVries's basic pie is open to your invention.

Pie crust for a 9" pie
1/2 lb Swiss cheese (shredded)
1 Tbs flour
2 Tbs olive oil
1 cup milk ("I like half 'n half")
3 eggs, very well beaten
2 medium onions, chopped
Salt and pepper to taste

○ Line pie dish with pastry.
○ Dredge cheese with flour (place shredded cheese in paper bag with flour and shake).
○ Cover bottom of pie shell with sautéed onions. Place flour coated cheese over onions. Drizzle with 2 Tbs olive oil.
○ Beat the eggs well, mix with milk or half 'n half and pour over cheese. Make sure the milk mix covers the cheese, but is not swimming.
○ Bake in 400 ° oven for 15 minutes. Insert knife in center. If it comes out clean, your pie is done. Serve hot. Serves 4 nicely.
○ In addition to the onions, use bacon, ham, crab, asparagus, or broccoli. For a great late night supper serve with a spinach salad. As an appetizer, just cut small wedges.

**Joyce DeVries**, wife of Tom DeVries, grandson of R. Hirt Jr, ran the Hirt catalog business before she and Tom retired. "Our three children worked at the business in some form or another while growing up. I worked at Hirt's off and on and began packing gift boxes in 1968 for selected clients. I became a manager of the R. Hirt, Jr., Co. Mail Order Division.

This recipe was given to me 30 years ago by a chef who was doing a demo at the Music Hall. I've used it over the years, and it's always a hit. Of course I use the shorter method, with a prepared pie crust and dried onions. "

*Notes*:

# Grits with Cheese and Eggs

For a light supper, served with a green salad, it makes a complete meal.

> 3/4 cup white grits
> 3 cups water
> 3/4 tsp salt
> 1/4 cup butter
> 1 cup cheese (Scottish Cheddar,
>     Vermont Cheddar, etc.),
>     grated
> 2 eggs, well beaten

○ Bring water to a boil and add salt. Stir in grits slowly and cook over low heat 2 to 5 minutes. Stir occasionally. Add butter and cheese. Stir until melted.

○ Stir in eggs; keep stirring until eggs are cooked. Serve immediately. Serves 4.

# Egg Strata

This is a flexible recipe. The proportions here are for serving 6, but it easily expands to feed a horde. Onions, mushrooms, and/or peppers can be sautéed and added to the drained, cooked sausage, or use ham instead of the sausage, or just use lots of vegetables and no meat. Keep the proportions of bread, eggs, and milk as they are here if you expand the dish.

*6 slices, cubed good quality firm white bread*
*1 lb sausage, cooked, crumbled, and*
      *well-drained*
*1 cup cheddar cheese, grated*
*6 eggs*
*2 cups milk*
*1 tsp salt*
*1 tsp dry mustard*

○ *Butter an 11"x7" baking dish. Cover bottom with bread cubes, distribute sausage evenly over bread, and cheese over sausage.*
○ *Mix well eggs, salt, and dry mustard and pour over bread and meat covering evenly. Cover with plastic wrap and refrigerate overnight.*
○ *Remove from refrigerator 1 hour before baking, unwrap, and bake at 350° for 45 minutes. Let rest 10 to 20 minutes before cutting into squares.*

# Pizza Rustica (meat)

*I*talian families have their favorite versions; this one is Berta Leone's. It is not the familiar pizza, but a meat pie traditionally served on Easter.

*Filling:*
*2 lbs Ricotta cheese*
*4 eggs*
*1/2 lb sweet Italian sausage, fried, cooled, and chopped*
*1/2 lb lean pork, cut into small cubes, fried, and cooled*
*1/2 cup grated Parmesan cheese*
*1/2 lb prosciutto ham, diced*
*1/2 lb Mozzarella cheese, cut into small cubes*
*1/2 cup finely chopped parsley*
*Pepper*

○ *Preheat oven to 400 °. Beat Ricotta cheese and eggs until smooth. Add remaining ingredients and mix well. Pour into 9"x9" pan, lined with pizza crust.*

*Pizza Crust:*
*2 cups sifted all-purpose flour*
*1/4 cup sugar\**

*2 tsp baking powder*
*1/2 cup butter or margarine*
*2 eggs*

○ *On pastry board or in a bowl, combine flour, sugar and baking powder. With fingers, break butter into flour until flour is mealy. Make a well in the flour and break the eggs into it; beat them with a fork. Blend into the flour mixture, and gather into a ball. Knead quickly. Let rest 10 minutes under a bowl. Dough tends to be soft, so it must be lightly floured on both sides as it is rolled out.*

○ *Using 2/3 of dough, roll out to fit a 9" round or 8" square pan with about 1/2" overhang. Pour mixture into pastry-lined pan. Roll out the remaining dough to cover the top. Trim the overhang and press edges with fork prongs. With fork, prick the top crust to allow steam to escape. Place in oven for 15 minutes, then reduce heat to 325° and cook 45-55 minutes longer. Turn off the heat and let cool in oven. Cut into 2" squares. Serve as a warm or cold hors d'oeuvre or as a luncheon dish. Yield: about 16 (2") pieces.*

*Editor's note:
This is the traditional amount of sugar, making a very sweet dough. Using 2 Tbs sugar will still give a sweetness and will also make the dough easier to roll out. The filling exactly filled a 9" round baking dish.

> **Berta Leone** gives credit to her mother-in-law, "a fabulous cook, whose enthusiasm, instruction and Market shopping skills, inspired and developed my culinary output."

# Baked Polynesian Corned Beef

Tom Wigley, owner of Wigley's Meats (p. 44), promises "we do such a fine job of curing the beef, you only need a pot of water to cook it in." Experiment with this baked glaze.

*1/2 cup mustard*
*3 Tbs brown sugar*
*Ginger ale*

◯ *Parboil beef for 2 1/2 hours in its original, unopened cooking bag. Remove from bag and place on a rack in a roasting pan, fat side up. Mix mustard and brown sugar. Score meat on both sides and spread with mixture. Add water to pan until it reaches the bottom of the rack. Baste with ginger ale. Place in 350° oven and roast 45 minutes or until well glazed. Cool slightly before slicing.*

# *Breaded Italian Meat Boats*

*A*nn Ciaramitaro (p. 41), wife of Sal Ciaramitaro often bakes these tasty meat loaves for family and friends. For an easy side dish, small par-boiled (10 minutes) new potatoes drizzled with olive oil can roast along with the boats.

> *2 lbs ground beef*
> *2 eggs*
> *1 1/2 Tbs finely chopped Italian parsley*
> *3 Tbs grated Parmesan cheese*
> *1 cup Italian seasoned breadcrumbs*
> *Milk to moisten*
> *1 1/2 tsp finely chopped tomato*
> *1 onion and 1 tomato, each sliced*

○ *Mix together well the meat, eggs, cheese, breadcrumbs, parsley, chopped tomato, and milk if necessary to hold mixture together. Form into oval-shaped meat loaves about 1" thick and 3" long. Brush each loaf with corn oil and roll them in the seasoned breadcrumbs. Place in a lightly greased baking dish, not crowded, and lay a slice of onion and tomato on each. Bake in a preheated 350° oven for 45 minutes until meat is done. Makes about 6 individual loaves or 12-15 appetizer loaves.*

Editor's note: We seasoned the meat mixture with 3/4 tsp salt and a few grindings of black pepper and brushed the little loaves with olive oil instead of corn oil. Very lean ground sirloin took 4-6 Tbs milk to moisten and lighten the meat mixture.

# Ganache Fassoulia

Michelle Andonian (p. 62), "the photographer lady," enjoys this classic Armenian green bean stew.

*2 to 4 lamb shanks*
*1 or 2 large onions, chopped*
*2 Tbs of olive oil*
*3 lbs green beans (washed and cut)*
*1 large can of stewed tomatoes*
          *(28-ounces)*
*1 can of tomato sauce (8-ounces)*
*1/2 to 1 cup of water*
*Salt and pepper to taste*
*A good loaf of bread*

○ *Brown meat and onions in olive oil. Add green beans, tomatoes (stewed and sauce), and enough water to cover. Let simmer about 2 hours until beans are tender. Add salt and pepper to taste.*

○ *You can use ground beef or ground turkey instead of lamb. If you do, be sure to add Worcestershire sauce and Maggi seasoning to give the turkey some flavor. Enjoy, and soak up the juice with that good bread. Serves 4.*

# Middle-Eastern Lamb

Spicy lamb patties, sautéed in a skillet, or even better, grilled over glowing coals, are perfect with Middle-Eastern Okra (p. 128).

*1 1/2 lbs lean, ground lamb*
*1 tsp salt*
*1 tsp ground cumin*
*1 large clove garlic, finely minced*
*Freshly ground black pepper*
*1/4 tsp hot red pepper flakes*
*1/4 tsp fresh mint, minced (optional)*
*Olive oil*

○ *Combine well all ingredients except oil. Shape into 4 ovals, then flatten, keeping oval shape. Lightly brush with oil. Grill or sauté over high heat, 3-4 minutes per side, until well-browned, but lightly pink and juicy inside.*

# Mustard-Baked Pork Chops

*For each 1" thick, well-trimmed pork loin
        chop, 6-8 ounces:*
*1 tsp Dijon mustard*
*2 cloves roasted garlic, mashed (p. 127)*
*1 1/2 tsp crushed cumin seeds or peppercorns*
*1/4 tsp salt*

○ *Pre-heat oven to 450 °. Combine mustard and garlic. Spread both sides of chops with mixture, then sprinkle with salt and press on crushed cumin or pepper. If using cumin, season also with a little freshly-ground pepper.*
○ *In heavy oven-going skillet, heat a film of canola oil over high heat. Brown chops 2 minutes on each side. Put skillet in oven and bake chops 12 minutes. Serve immediately.*

*Notes:*

# Veal Scaloppine a la Tosca

A favorite at Roma Cafe (p. 33).

8 pieces veal cutlet
Salt and pepper
2 eggs
1/2 cup half and half
2 Tbs Parmesan cheese
1 garlic clove, minced
1 tsp parsley, chopped
Flour
Olive oil or corn oil

○ Pound meat to medallion size. Salt and pepper each side. Beat eggs; add cream, cheese, garlic, and parsley. Pat meat in flour, then dip in egg mixture. Heat oil, enough to cover bottom of largest skillet by 1/8" until very hot but not smoking. Sauté in oil until meat is brown on both sides. (Approximately 5 minutes total for both sides.)

# Eastern Market Deviled Baked Chicken

All the ingredients in our *Eastern Market Deviled Baked Chicken* come from the Market.

> *3 cups fresh white breadcrumbs*
> *1 cup freshly grated Parmesan cheese*
> *1/2 cup minced fresh Italian parsley*
> *2 Tbs Rafal's HOT "Salt Free" Cajun Seasoning*
> *1 Tbs sweet Paprika*
> *1 Tbs dried Greek oregano*
> *2 tsp salt*
> *1 tsp freshly ground pepper*
> *1 cup butter, melted*
> *1/2 cup Dijon mustard*
> *18-24 assorted chicken pieces*

○ *Trim any excess fat from chicken, wash, and dry on paper towels. Combine melted butter with Dijon mustard. Combine all dry ingredients in large, flat dish. Brush chicken pieces completely with mustard mixture, coat on all sides with breadcrumb mixture and put on jelly roll pans that have been lightly greased. Don't crowd the pieces. Put breasts and wings on one sheet, drumsticks and thighs on a second one. Cover loosely with waxed paper and refrigerate. It's best to do this early in the day.*

◯ *Thirty minutes before cooking, preheat oven to 350° and take chicken from refrigerator. Bake for one hour until golden brown and tender, alternating pans and removing breasts' pan when they are done (small boneless pieces won't take as long as big breast halves with bone). Serve warm or at room temperature.*

◯ *Like all breaded foods, this chicken is better before being refrigerated. Count on at least two pieces per guest, and serve with a well-chilled white wine or ice-cold lemonade. Enjoy!*

# Roasted Turkey Dressing
## (meat)

Lil Arnone (p. 24) loves to cook and would rather entertain at her table than eat out. Her Italian-style turkey, with the family's traditional sausage stuffing, is hardy.

*2 Tbs butter*
*4 Tbs olive oil*
*1/2 cup chopped onions*
*1/2 cup chopped celery*
*4 cups cooked rice*
*3 lbs Rinaldi Italian Sausage*
*2 cups seasoned Italian breadcrumbs*
*3/4 cup grated Parmesan cheese*
*2 eggs*
*Chicken stock, about 1/2 cup*

○ *Sauté onions and celery in butter and 2 Tbs olive oil until transparent. Remove from pan and combine with cooked rice. Add breadcrumbs and cheese and salt and pepper to taste. Add last 2 Tbs oil to pan.*

○ *Remove sausage from casings and cook until all pink is gone, breaking up sausage with fork as it cooks. Drain sausage well in a colander. When cool, add to rice mixture. Beat eggs and add, mixing well. Add just enough broth to hold the dressing together. This is sufficient to stuff a 15-18 lb turkey, with a little left over to bake separately. Other seasonings can be added, such as poultry*

seasoning or sage, or 1/2 cup of chopped fresh
Italian parsley.

Editor's note:  To serve as a supper
casserole, bake in a greased 9"x12"
pan at 400 ° for 45-60 minutes.

*Roasted Turkey:*

○  Wash  thoroughly,  pat  dry,  and  rub
turkey cavity with a cut clove of garlic.  Stuff just
before roasting.  If you wish to baste your turkey,
melt 1/2 cup butter and add 1 smashed clove of
garlic, 1/2 tsp paprika, and the juice of 1/2 lemon.
○  Roast turkey at 350 °, 15-18 minutes
per  pound  for  turkey  under  12  pounds,  12-14
minutes per pound for larger turkey.  Thigh jucies
should run clear; meat thermometer should read
170-175 °.

# Microwaved Asparagus

In June, when pencil-thin asparagus is available, try this easy cooking method. It also works for sugar-snap peas, plentiful in June and July.

○ *Wash the pencil-thin asparagus well to remove sand, break off woody ends, and place neatly in a freezer zip-lock bag. Seal the bag all but 2 inches and microwave at full power for 3 minutes. Snip off the lower corner of bag to drain excess water, turn onto a platter, season and serve.*

# Green Beans with Smoked Turkey Wings

Lucille (Willis) Coles's (p. 57) special recipe for green beans and turkey wings.

2 lbs green beans
1 lbs smoked turkey wings*
2-3 cloves peeled garlic, optional

◯ Cook turkey wings in small amount of water for 45 minutes. Wash and snap beans while wings are cooking. Take turkey from broth and remove skin. Strain and defat water. Return water to pot and add beans. Cook 45 minutes longer. Season to taste with salt and pepper.
◯ Serve beans with or without turkey meat.

*Editor's note:
Smoked turkey legs are meatier and have less fat.

# Roasted Beets and Garlic with Balsamic Vinaigrette

Beets are plentiful from August on.

○ *Select 2"-3" medium-sized beets (with their tops on).\* Remove the tops and long roots, wash and pat dry, and place the beets in the center of a large sheet of aluminum foil. Scatter unpeeled cloves or garlic, one clove per beet, over them, drizzle with a little olive oil, sprinkle with salt and black pepper. Fold the foil butcher-wrap style to make an airtight package but that leaves a little room for steam expansion.*

○ *Roast the beets in a 400 ° oven until tender. While timing depends on the size and age of the beets and your oven temperature, an hour is usually long enough. (Be careful of escaping steam when you open the packet to see if they are tender.)*

○ *When the beets are cool enough to handle but still quite warm, hold the beets on the tines of a cooking fork to peel them. Slice or cube them into a bowl.*

○ *To make the vinaigrette, squeeze the roasted garlic into a small bowl, mash with a fork, add extra olive oil and any remaining oil from the packet and 1 Tbs dark balsamic vinegar. Salt and pepper to taste.*

○ *Toss the beets with the dressing and garnish with minced parsley or chives. Serve warm or at room temperature. The beets keep well in the refrigerator for 2 or 3 days. Bring to room temperature to serve.*

*Editor's note:
Never buy beets without tops. Fresh green tops insure this year's crop.

*Notes:*

# Marty Rafal's Kosher Dills

Making pickles is an annual Rafal (p. 27) family event, using Donald's father's formula.

*Firm cucumbers (washed)*
*Garlic cloves*
*Fresh dill*
*Mixed pickling spices*
*10 quarts HOT water*
*1 cup Kosher salt*
*1/2 cup sugar*
*1/2 cup white vinegar*

○ *Place cucumbers in sterilized jars. To each jar, add 1 to 2 cloves of garlic, coarsely chopped, and 2 tsp mixed pickling spices and fresh dill sprigs.*
○ *Make a brine by dissolving vinegar, salt, sugar, and hot water. Pour brine over contents of jars filling each to within 1" of top. Cover tightly. Keep in cool dark place 2 to 4 weeks.*
○ *Store in refrigerator up to 2 months.*

# Roasted Garlic

Roast garlic when the oven is heated for something else and refrigerate after it cools a bit. In an airtight bag, it keeps a week or more.

Roasted garlic freezes well. Peel individual roasted cloves and place in a small freezer ziplock bag, seal, expelling as much air as possible. They defrost in seconds and can be sliced paper-thin in their semi-thawed state.

*To bake a whole head of garlic:*

○ *Pull off any loose outer skin and slice off the top 1/8". Place garlic on a square of heavy-duty foil, or in a terra cotta garlic roaster, drizzle with 2 Tbs olive oil, and seal tightly. Bake at 400° for 45 minutes until soft when pierced with a knife.*

# Middle-Eastern Okra

This delicious recipe for okra evolved from an exchange of cooking ideas at the Market. With spicy lamb patties (p. 115) and couscous it makes a flavorful entrée year-round.

*1 1/2 lbs small okra*
*2 medium onions, thinly sliced*
*4 cloves garlic, thinly sliced*
*Fresh or dried basil*
*1/4 cup extra-virgin olive oil*
*Salt and freshly ground black pepper, to*
*taste*
*6 to 8 Roma tomatoes, washed and sliced in*
*1/4" rounds*

○ *Wash okra in large amount of cold water. Snip off the stem tip but don't cut into okra and expose seeds. Drain and pat dry.*

○ *In large, non-stick skillet, heat olive oil over medium-high heat. Add sliced onions and sauté, stirring 5 minutes. Add garlic and cook another minute. Add okra and sauté, lifting and tossing in oil, until okra turns bright green. Sprinkle with salt and pepper and lower heat. Cover okra with a tight layer of tomato slices, lightly salt and pepper, and sprinkle with basil, preferably fresh. Drizzle tomatoes with an extra spoonful of olive oil, if desired.*

○ Select a lid slightly smaller than the skillet that will fit inside the skillet and weight down the okra, but allows steam to escape around the edges. Cook, undisturbed, over low heat for 30-40 minutes, until okra is very tender. If the dish is soupy, uncover for the last 5 minutes to reduce to a syrupy consistency.

○ To serve, select a platter or shallow bowl, and tilt skillet, sliding okra onto it, keeping the tomato layer on top. This dish is good at all temperatures, but at its best, slightly warm. Serves 4.

**Notes:**

# Pumpkin Gratin

Try pumpkin as a vegetable for your Thanksgiving feast. It's a natural with turkey, but would complement a luscious pork roast.

*3 garlic cloves, minced*
*1/3 cup extra-virgin olive oil*
*4 cups pumpkin, peeled, sliced and*
            *diced into 1/2" cubes (The small pie*
            *pumpkins are best for this.)*
*3 Tbs flour*
*1/2 cup grated Parmesan cheese*
*1/2 tsp salt and some freshly-ground black*
            *pepper*
*1/4 cup minced Italian parsley*
*1/2 tsp dried thyme*

○ *Combine all ingredients in large bowl and mix well. Bake in a well-oiled, 1 1/2 quart shallow baking dish in a 325° oven for 1 1/2 hours, until cheese is lightly browned and pumpkin is done. Sprinkle with a little extra parsley and serve to four.*

# Fried Green Tomatoes

When the first frost of autumn threatens, farmers gather in their fully formed but still green tomatoes. Many relishes, chutneys, and jams are put up. If you don't have that much time, fry slices and serve with baked pork chops.

4 green tomatoes
Salt
Rafal's Hot Cajun Seasoning
1/2 cup flour
3 Tbs cornmeal
Rendered bacon fat and/or olive oil

○ Slice hard green tomatoes in 1/4" slices. Lay out on waxed paper, sprinkle each side with salt and Cajun Seasoning.
○ Combine flour and cornmeal.
○ Heat heavy skillet over high heat with 2 Tbs each rendered bacon fat and olive oil. (You can use all oil, but don't expect the same flavor.) Dip tomato slices, one at a time, in flour mixture to coat both sides and slide into hot oil. Fry 4 minutes a side. Drain well and serve hot.

# Sauerkraut and Kielbasa

This wonderful marriage of fermented and fresh cabbage, seasoned with Polish sausage, has been passed on through Kristine Lessins's family members and friends. She uses only top-quality meat market sausage.

*1 head fresh green cabbage, cored and thinly sliced*
*1 package refrigerated sauerkraut, well rinsed and drained*
*3 cloves garlic, minced*
*1 1/2-2 lbs. fresh or smoked kielbasa, or a combination, pricked well so they won't burst during baking*

○ *Cook cabbage in boiling water until tender, drain well, and mix with drained kraut and minced garlic. Season with salt and pepper.*
○ *Place mixture in a lightly greased baking dish (13" x 9") and top with sausages. Bake at 350 ° for 45-60 minutes, or until sausages are done, turning them after 25 minutes to brown both sides. Loosely cover dish with foil if it seems to be getting dry or if sausages need to cook more thoroughly. Serves 6.*

Kris and Jerry Lessins have been coming to the Market since they were teenagers. In the 1960's as a young married couple, they made the Market their weekly shopping trip with their sons. Today, Matt and his wife bring the next generation to the Market.

# Canning and Putting-by

Preserving the harvest's bounty is a time-honored tradition still observed. Most Eastern Market farmers will share canning or pickling recipes when asked. Besides being practical (it's generally impossible to eat all the ripe produce at its peak), food preserving provides a satisfying end to the growing cycle--a time to reflect and to get a last ounce of enjoyment and flavor out of the season.

Canned goods last longest. Many pickles and jams are actually better the second year. The process is easy, but certain rules must be followed. All jars and rings must be washed and sterilized (the hottest setting on most dishwashers is sufficient). The jars must be hot and the food going into them must also be hot when they are filled. The glass rim of the jar must be clean and dry for the rubber ringed lid to seal. Filled and capped jars are then submerged in boiling water and simmered for the time specified in the recipe (from 5 to 20 minutes). The processed jars must then cool at room temperature. As the small amount of air in the jars contracts, the lids will "ping." If they don't, it is best to refrigerate those jars and use them within a month. Canned foods should be kept in a cool, dark place.

With today's heavy, plastic freezer bags and containers, freezing may be the least time-consuming of any preserving method. Sterilizing isn't necessary. But frozen foods' shelf life isn't as long as canned, three to twelve months, and defrosting takes time when you want to use the foods.   Expelling as much air as possible before closing containers, and freezing only well-cleaned foods at their peak is important for maximum flavor.   Baked goods and cooked soups freeze well, as do small, whole foods like Roma tomatoes and ripe berries.

Drying fruits and vegetables (a common practice before refrigeration) is again popular.   Once the food is cleaned and cut, time and patience are the only requirements.  Food dehydrators make drying easy.

Recommended reading for food preservation:

Stocking Up, 3rd edition, by Carol Hupping for Rodale Books.  Simon & Schuster, Inc. New York. 1986.

Complete Guide to Home Canning, Preserving and Freezing, United States Department of Agriculture. Dover Publication, Inc. New York. 1973.

# Chow Chow

John D. Hill (p. 57) puts up his family recipe for Chow Chow using his fresh Michigan vegetables.

*Place in crock overnight:*
*1 large cauliflower (in florets)*
*6 cucumbers, cubed (leave peel on)*
*2 lbs pickling onions*
*4 large peppers (2 red, 2 green) cubed*
*1/2 cup pickling salt, sprinkled over*

○ *Next day drain, do not rinse, and place in large kettle.*

*Sauce:*
*Mix to make paste:*
*3/4 cup water*
*3 cup brown sugar, packed*
*1 cup flour*
*3 Tbs dry mustard*
*1 Tbs tumeric*

*Add to paste:*
*2 quarts boiling cider vinegar*

○ *Add mixture to vegetables and boil 4 minutes. Watch and stir gently, constantly! Place in hot, sterilized jars and seal.\**

*Editor's note: Ideally, if jars and mixtures are very hot, the lids will seal (listen for the "ping" of the lid contracting). If they don't seal, refrigerate and use within a month.

# Ratatouille Niçoise

  There are probably as many varieties of ratatouille (ra-ta-twee-ah) as there are villages in the Provence region of France, and this unusual freezer method gives excellent results.

  1/2 cup olive oil, divided
  2 cups coarsely chopped onions
  2 Tbs finely chopped garlic
  1 eggplant*, peeled and cut in 1" cubes,
     about 4 cups
  2 peppers, red or green, in 1" cubes, 2 cups
  6 small zucchini (or mixed summer squashes),
     in 1" cubes, 4 cups
  1 bay leaf
  1/2 tsp dried thyme or a few sprigs of fresh
  16-18 Italian plum tomatoes, peeled
     and cubed
  1/8 tsp dried hot red pepper flakes
  24 imported black olives, pitted and halved
     (Kalamata or Niçoise)
  24 green olives, preferably Picholine, pitted
     and halved
  1/2 cup each, minced Italian flat leaf
     parsley and basil
  Salt and pepper to taste

○ Heat half of the olive oil in a large, heavy skillet or Dutch oven. Add onions and garlic and cook until soft. Add eggplant and cook five minutes, stirring often. Add the rest of oil and peppers, cook and stir a minute and add zucchini. Add salt and pepper to taste. Add bay leaf and thyme and cook 5 minutes, stirring occasionally. Add tomatoes and hot pepper flakes and bring to a simmer. Add olives, parsley, and basil. Cover and cook gently for 10 minutes. At this point, the vegetables will not be fully cooked.

○ Cool the ratatouille quickly by setting pan in ice water and stirring occasionally. (Keep a little out to have for that night's supper.) Spoon it into plastic freezer containers or bags leaving head space for expansion. Seal tightly and freeze.

○ When ready to use, thaw in refrigerator overnight. Simmer or bake, uncovered, for 30 minutes until all vegetables are tender. Makes 10-12 cups.

*Editors note:
Before cooking eggplant, taste a cube and if bitter, salt it and drain in a colander until it gives up its brown liquid. Rinse, pat dry, and proceed with your recipe.

# Pickled Green Beans

In the Haack (p. 54) family, Pickled Green Beans are a favorite of the college generation--a great snack food to take back to school.  Use only young, tender beans.

Green beans, washed and ends trimmed
Garlic cloves, peeled
1/4 tsp hot seasoning spices, per pint
7 cups vinegar
7 cups water
2/3 cup kosher salt
Fresh dill sprigs

○ Place 1 dill sprig, 1 garlic clove, 1/4 tsp hot seasoning spices in bottom of each hot, sterilized pint canning jar.  Pack each jar tightly and vertically with green beans, filling as full as possible.  Bring vinegar, water, and salt to a boil and fill each jar.  Clean rims of jars, seal immediately, and put into hot water bath, with water to cover.  Boil jars 15 minutes.  Remove from water bath and place on toweling or cooling racks.  (If you set hot jars on a cold surface they might crack.)  Let cool completely before storing.  Refrigerate remaining pickling solution to use for future batches.  (makes approximately 12 pints)

**June Haack** (Haack Farm Produce) gives advice on canning home-grown vegetables. Wash and sterilize your canning jars. Make up your pickling solution. As vegetables are ready to be canned, reheat the jars in a 200° oven for 10 minutes and soak the rubber rimmed lids in boiling water. Fill the hot jars with prepared vegetables, bring the pickling solution to a boil and pour into jars filling within 1/4" of rim. Seal and process in water bath. This allows you to can smaller quantities at a time so you don't need a whole day set aside for the task.

*Notes:*

# Pear/Raspberry Jam

In early fall, we get a second chance to enjoy raspberries.

6 medium pears (2 lbs) peeled, cored and
        coarsely chopped
10 ounces raspberries (fresh or frozen)
6 cups sugar
2 Tbs lemon juice
2 tsp orange peel, grated
1 pouch liquid pectin

○ Add enough pears to raspberries to make 4 cups. Combine them well with sugar, lemon juice and orange peel in a heavy kettle. Bring to a full boil, stirring constantly, and boil 1 minute, still stirring constantly. Remove from heat and stir in pectin. Skim off all foam.
○ Ladle into hot, sterilized 1/2 pint jars, leaving 1/4" headspace. Wipe rims, adjust lids. Process in boiling water 15 minutes. Makes 6 to 7 half-pints.

**Denise Scott**, a Market shopper for over twenty-five years, makes her Pear/Raspberry jam in the fall because Bartlett pears are also in season and will ripen quickly if stored in a brown paper bag for a day or two.

# Dried Herb Tips

Here are some tips from Shirley Jentzen (p. 54) on how to dry herbs. She thinks the faster the drying time, the greener the end product.

*Using a microwave:*
○ *Lay out a single layer of herbs\* on paper towel. Microwave on high for only a second or two. Turn herbs and repeat process until herbs are dry.*

*Using a gas oven:*
○ *Put your herbs on a cookie sheet, in a single layer. Don't light the oven. Keep turning until dry.*

○ *Hanging herbs upside down:*
*It is not necessary for them to be in the dark. Take the rubber band off once they are dry so the herbs will not mold.*

\*Editor's note:
Always wash all your herbs, even those from your own garden.

# Beet Cake

If you offer this cake to guests, present a prize to the one who guesses the unusual but delicious ingredients. Offered by Helen Penzien (p. 55).

2 cups sugar
1 cup oil
2 eggs
2 tsp vanilla
1 teaspoon salt
1 cup chopped nuts* (optional)
2 tsp cinnamon
2 tsp soda
2 1/2 cups flour, sifted
1 cup cooked diced beets, drained
1 cup cottage cheese
1 cup crushed pineapple, drained

○ Put sugar, oil, eggs, and vanilla in large mixing bowl. Stir 2 minutes. Stir in cottage cheese, pineapple, and beets.
○ Sift together flour, baking soda, salt, and cinnamon. Add dry ingredients and nuts to batter. Mix thoroughly for 4 minutes. Turn batter into greased and floured 13"x9" pan. Bake at 350° approximately 50-60 minutes, until toothpick inserted in center comes out clean. Cool cake thoroughly in pan.

*Editor's note:
Toasting nuts increases their flavor in baked goods.   Ten
minutes at 350° is usually sufficient.   Watch carefully.
Dredging dry fruit or nuts with a little flour before adding to a
cake-type batter keeps them from sinking to the bottom of the
cake while baking.

Notes:

# Carrot Cake

ℛ Sawicki (p. 53) family favorite, carrot cake, uses only their organic carrots.

*3 cups flour*
*2 tsp baking powder*
*2 tsp baking soda*
*1 tsp salt*
*2 tsp cinnamon*
*1 2/3 cup oil*
*3 cups grated carrots*
*4 eggs*
*1/2 cup chopped walnuts*
*2 cups sugar*
*3/4 cup diced pineapple (optional)*

○ *Sift flour once. Sift again twice with baking powder, cinnamon, baking soda, and salt into a bowl.*

○ *Combine sugar and oil. Add eggs one at a time, mixing well after each. Thoroughly fold in dry ingredients. Fold in carrots, walnuts, and pineapple.*

○ *Pour into a well-greased 10" tube pan. Bake in 350° oven for 1 hour, or until tester comes out clean.*

# Holiday Torte

For her Holiday Torte, Kay Kravutske makes use of the wide choice of apples at the Market. Her mother's recipe uses Northern Spy or any variety of juicy cooking apples.

4 cups peeled diced apples
1 cup sugar
1/2 cup flour
2 tsp baking powder
1 egg beaten
1 Tbs melted butter
1 tsp vanilla
1/2 cup chopped walnuts
1/2 cup chopped dates

○ Mix dry ingredients together, add to fruits and nuts.
○ Add vanilla and butter to egg, and stir into fruit mixture. Mix well. Pour into a greased 8x8" baking pan. Bake at 400° for 40 minutes. Serve warm with vanilla ice cream or whipped cream. Serves 6.

**Kay Kravutske**, an excellent cook, has shopped the Market for years. She loves to bake for her large family.

# Tarte Tatin

The ultimate apple pie. This upside-down tart condenses four and a half pounds of apples into an inch-thick carmelized marmalade.

Crust:
2 cups flour
1/3 cup sugar
Pinch of salt
1 stick unsalted butter, diced
2 eggs

Filling:
1 stick unsalted butter
3/4 cup sugar
4 1/2 lbs Golden Delicious apples

○ Make crust by mixing dry ingredients together, then cutting in the butter either with fingertips, food processor, or mixer until crumbly. Beat eggs. Add 3/4 of eggs to dry mixture, mixing until dough forms. If necessary, add more egg by drops. Knead dough four or five turns by hand and form into a flat cake. Place on square of waxed paper, top with another square of paper and roll out dough, from center to edges, turning to keep round, until dough is diameter of waxed paper square. Refrigerate.

○ For filling, prepare an 11" heavy oven-going skillet (preferably cast iron) by slicing butter thinly and covering bottom of skillet with slices in close-fitting rounds. Sprinkle sugar evenly over butter. Wash, peel, halve, and core apples. Cut each half in sixths, and arrange apple slices attractively, in circles, over sugar for first layer. Then evenly pile rest of apple slices in skillet. On top of stove, place skillet over medium heat and cook 30 minutes until juices are amber-colored. Remove from heat and using a bulb baster, draw off 4-5 Tbs butter-sugar juices and place in a small non-stick skillet. Reserve.

○ Take dough from refrigerator, remove top waxed paper, and invert dough onto apples. Peel off waxed paper, tuck in edges, and cut slits in dough to let steam escape. Bake tart in middle of pre-heated 375° oven 30 to 45 minutes until top is golden. Remove from oven, let rest a few minutes and invert skillet over large flat plate. Let rest and settle a few minutes again, then lift off skillet. Using narrow spatula, replace any apple slices that stuck to skillet.

○ Over medium heat, boil down reserved juices until syrupy then drizzle over apples. Serve warm or at room temperature. It is even better the next day. Don't refrigerate, just cover with plastic wrap. Serves 10-12.

# Strawberry/Rhubarb Pie

Strawberries and rhubarb go together like tomatoes and basil. In Michigan, they are in the Market together in June. California berries will do in a pinch, but Michigan rhubarb is essential.

*Your favorite 2-crust pie dough*
*2 1/2 cups Michigan strawberries, washed and*
*stemmed*
*2 1/2 cups rhubarb, washed and cut in 1"*
*pieces*
*1 1/2 cups sugar*
*1/4 tsp salt*
*6 Tbs flour*
*2 1/2 Tbs cold butter, diced*

○ *Combine fruits. Combine dry ingredients well. Line 9" pie plate with 1/2 of rolled-out pastry, letting extra dough hang over plate. Cover with 1/2 fruit mixture, sprinkle with 1/2 sugar mixture; repeat. Dot with butter.*
○ *Place other half of rolled dough over filling. Seal edges carefully, folding lower dough over upper and crimping well. Cut a few slits or a pretty design in top dough to let steam escape. If desired, brush with a little milk and sprinkle with extra sugar. Bake in preheated 425 ° oven for 40-50 minutes.*

# Peanut Butter Cookies

This recipe, developed by Patrick Krekreghe (p.47), owner of Beans R Us, puts his bean flour to interesting use.

*1 1/2 cups all-purpose flour*
*1 cup bean flour*
*1 1/2 tsp salt*
*1 1/2 tsp baking soda*
*1 cup smooth peanut butter*
*1 cup margarine\**
*1 cup white sugar*
*1 cup dark brown sugar*
*1 whole egg and 1 egg white*
*1 tsp pure vanilla*
*2 cups real chocolate chips (optional)*

○ *Mix flours, salt, and soda and set aside. Cream well margarine, peanut butter, and both sugars. Add egg, egg white, and vanilla. Blend well. Stir in flour mixture (mixture will be stiff).*

○ *Chill dough for at least 1/2 hour. Drop dough from 2" scoop onto parchment paper-lined cookie sheet. Flatten cookies with fork dipped in flour. Bake at 350° for 6-7 minutes.\*\* Do not over-bake. The bottom of the cookie should be lightly browned. Cookies should be chewy and moist.*

\*Editor's note: We used 1/2 cup butter and 1/4 cup Sunsweet "Lighter Bake" to reduce fat content.
\*\*Editor's note: Our cookies baked in 11-13 minutes.

# Sour Cream Twists

Dorothy Karpus has made these pastries for her family and drop-in guests for over sixty years.

*4 cups flour*
*1 tsp salt*
*1 cup shortening\**
*1 envelope quick dry yeast*
*1/4 cup lukewarm water*
*1 egg*
*2 egg yolks*
*1 cup sour cream*
*1 tsp vanilla*
*3/4 cup sugar*

○ *Sift 4 cups flour and salt into a bowl. Cut in 1 cup of shortening, as for pie crust. Soak 1 envelope quick dry yeast in 1/4 cup lukewarm water, according to directions on the envelope. Beat 1 egg and 2 egg yolks together. Combine with sour cream, yeast, and vanilla. Add to dry ingredients and mix thoroughly. Let rise in the refrigerator for 2 hours.*

○ *Sprinkle sugar lightly on a breadboard. Place dough on sugar. Sprinkle sugar lightly over dough and roll out into a 10" square. Fold dough in to center from either side. Roll out and repeat the folding, using a little more sugar. Do this two more times--four times in all--sprinkling sugar on the board and on dough each time to prevent sticking. Cut into strips 3/4" wide and 4" long. Sprinkle with sugar. Shape into twists by twisting the strips three or four times and place on ungreased cookie sheets several inches apart. Bake at 375 ° for 20-25 minutes, until golden brown. Makes 3 dozens twists.*

*Editor's note: Unsalted butter gives these pastries a wonderful flavor.

**Dorothy Karpus** remembers the Eastern Market as one of many family excursions with her husband and children. After an afternoon lunch at the Roma Cafe they would always take a stroll through the Market.

# Rhubarb Nut Bread

Carol Agocs's (p. 61) snacking cake from her mother.

1 1/2 cup brown sugar
2/3 cup oil
1 egg
1 cup soured milk*
1 tsp salt
1 tsp baking soda
1 tsp vanilla
2 1/2 cups all-purpose flour
1 1/2 cup diced rhubarb
1/2 cup walnuts, chopped

○ Combine sugar and oil; stir in egg with soured milk and vanilla. Add sifted dry ingredients (I sometimes add cinnamon and nutmeg for a spicy flavor). Stir in rhubarb and nuts. Pour into two greased loaf pans.

Topping:
1/2 cup sugar
1/2 tsp cinnamon
1 Tbs melted butter

○ Mix together and sprinkle over batter.

○ Bake at 325 °, 40-50 minutes, until toothpick inserted in center comes out clean. Let cool well before removing from pans.

*Editor's note:
To sour milk, add 1 tsp vinegar to 1 cup milk, let sit at room temperature 1 hour, or substitute 1 cup buttermilk.

# Zucchini Bread

June Haack's, of Haack Farm Produce (p. 54), favorite bread.

3 eggs
1 cup vegetable oil
2 cups sugar
2 tsp vanilla
3 cups flour
1 tsp salt
2 tsp baking soda
1/4 tsp baking powder
1 1/2 tsp cinnamon
3/4 tsp nutmeg
2 cups grated zucchini
8 ounce can crushed pineapple, drained
1 cup walnuts, chopped
1 cup raisins

○ Mix together eggs, oil, sugar, and vanilla. Sift together dry ingredients and add them alternately to egg mixture with zucchini and pineapple.

○ Put mixture in 2 well-greased 9"x5" loaf pans and bake in preheated 350° oven for 1 hour or until toothpick inserted in center comes out clean. Cool in pans 10-15 minutes before removing to wire rack to cool completely. This bread freezes well.

# ❧ Market Menus ☙

   Putting together dishes to comprise a full menu is often the most difficult task of cooking.  The season, the group to feed, the budget, and preparation time, determine ones choices.

   The menus given are sketches--easy to change, to add personal favorites.  All are offered in the spirit of the book: the joys of eating and cooking the best a farmers market has to offer.

# Spring

---

### A Mediterranean Feast

Shangleesh as an appetizer (p. 72)
CŞ
Middle-Eastern Lamb (p. 115) and Okra (p. 128)
Cumin-scented Couscous
Tabbooleh (p. 89)
CŞ
Carrot Cake (p. 144)

---

### Sunday Lunch

Baked Artichoke Dip (p. 73)
with toasted French bread rounds
CŞ
Egg Strata  (p. 109)
Tender, slender Asparagus (p. 122)
Warm dinner rolls
CŞ
Strawberry/Rhubarb Pie (p. 148)

# Summer

---

## Patio Party

Spinach/Strawberry Salad (p. 90)
ଔ
Grilled Chicken with Cajun Marinade (p. 99)
Corn on the Cob
Refrigerator Pickles (p. 88)
ଔ
Frozen Vanilla Yogurt
with Warm Ginger Plum Sauce (p. 98)

---

## Belle Isle Picnic

Tomato and Red Onion Salad (p. 91)
Crusty Italian Bread
ဢ
Eastern Market Deviled Baked Chicken (p. 118)
Rafal's Dill Pickles (p. 126)
Coleslaw Made Easy (p. 87)
ဢ
Lemonade
ဢ
Peanut Butter Cookies (p. 149)
Melonball Compôte (p. 92)

# Autumn

---

### Fireside Supper

Cajun Pumpkin Bisque with Shrimp (p. 78)
ↄჳ
Mustard-Baked Pork Chops (p. 116)
Fried Green Tomatoes (p. 131)
Wild Rice Salad (p. 93)
ↄჳ
Sour Cream Twists (p. 150)

---

### A Family Dinner

Warm Roquefort/Bacon Spread with Toasts (p. 71)
ↄჳ
Smoked Turkey Wings with Green Beans (p. 123)
Chow Chow (p. 135)
ↄჳ
Beet Cake (p. 142)

# *Winter*

---

## *All-in-the-Oven Supper*

Baked Mushrooms with Pesto (p. 74)

303

Italian Meat Boats (p. 113)
Pan-roasted Potatoes
Roasted Beets & Garlic with Balsamic Vinaigrette (p. 124)

303

Holiday Torte  (p. 145)

---

## *Festive Holiday Dinner*

Minestrone with Kale (p. 82)

303

Veal Scaloppine a la Tosca (p. 117)
Penne with Roasted Garlic Pesto (p. 94)
Baby Greens Salad with Orange/Lemon Thyme
Vinegar (p. 96) & Olive Oil Vinaigrette

303

Tarte Tatin (p. 146)

# ❦ Businesses Index ❧

# ↜ Recipe Index ↝

Recipe contributor code:

| | |
|---|---|
| F-*farmer* | RO-*restaurant owner* |
| MC-*market customer* | SO-*store owner* |
| ME-*market employee* | LJ-*Lois Johnson* |
| PD-*produce dealer* | MT-*Margaret Thomas* |

# ❧ *Last Thoughts* ❧

Detroit's Eastern Market is many things to many people. For Saul Wineman, "the Market is a place of joy." For some, it's where they grew up, worked with their parents, met their future spouses, and raised their children. For others, it's their neighborhood.

For thousands, it's our Saturday place where we come together, stock our larders and renew our spirits. It brings us in contact with our neighbors in a way that can't be found in a crowded, noisy, over-air-conditioned supermarket. If our produce is a little limp when we get home on a hot Saturday afternoon, we know it's hot with heat and not radiation. If we have to park and walk a block, there's always something interesting to catch our eye. We get to choose our own produce, see it in natural light, smell it. The Market reminds us there is a natural cycle, the growing seasons, something often forgotten in our busy city habitat.

To the City of Detroit, Eastern Market remains a great asset. Often controversial, generating diverse ideas for expansion or change, it is a necessity to our community and an enrichment to our lives.